HOTTEST STOCK CAR DRIVERS

Today's Greatest Superstars

Glenda J. Fordham

OVER
TIME
BOOKS

The Publisher: OverTime Books is an imprint of Éditions de
   la Montagne Verte

Library and Archives Canada Cataloguing in Publication

Fordham, Glenda J., 1953–
   Hottest stock car drivers : today's greatest superstars /
   Glenda J. Fordham.

   Includes bibliographical references.
   ISBN 13: 978-1-897277-04-1
   ISBN 10: 1-897277-04-0

   1. Stock car drivers—Biography. 2. Stock car drivers—United
States—Biography. I. Title.

GV1032.A1F67 2006   796.72'0922   C2006-902553-3

Project Director: J. Alexander Poulton

Cover Image: Jeff Gordon. Courtesy of Reuters/Corbis, photo by Brent Smith.

Title Page Image: Michael Gold. Courtesy of Allan Gold.

PC:P5

Dedication

This book is dedicated to Greg Biffle and
the No. 16 National Guard team,
whose 2005 Cup championship run
inspired me to write this book, and
to young CASCAR driver Michael Gold,
whose tenacity and hard work
will hopefully pay off one day
when he gets to go to "the big show."

Contents

Acknowledgments

I'd like to extend my heartfelt gratitude to a number of people, without whom I could not have embarked upon this wild ride, and whose support and encouragement got me to the literary checkered flag!

Thanks to my editor, the best crew chief a writer could have; my number one cheerleader, Jaclyn Solomon, for her constant flow of positive messages that she took time to deliver in the middle of her own personal "big wrecks"; Irene Trester, who made sure my fuel tanks were filled when I needed to get back off pit row; Jacqueline Robichaud, my dearest and oldest friend, who has always been there cheering me on down the backstretch; Heather Boyd, for her constant good humor and allowing me to vent when technology nearly sent me to the garage for good; and A.J. Cavanaugh, Michael Williams, Cathy D., Nik Beat and Roben Goodfellow, all of whom made sure I had all the tools I needed to drive this book into Victory Lane.

Introduction

In November, as I watched Tony Stewart secure his second championship title in the final race of the 2005 NASCAR Nextel Cup Series on TV, I realized how much I'd learned about the history of stock car racing, engine technology, track layout, race strategy and the meaning of bump-drafting over time. I'd spent weekends watching my heroes hurtle around racetracks at 170-plus miles per hour, gritting my teeth as my favorite drivers got caught up in the big wrecks and sitting on the edge of my couch as the checkered flag came out with two or three cars only fractions of a second apart as they raced to the finish line.

But it's the drivers themselves who pulled me into this world of heart-pounding speed and action. These are today's gladiators for whom we cheer and applaud. These are the new boys of summer, stars of multi-million-dollar sponsorship contracts, promotional deals and TV commercials. These are the good guys and the bad boys with dedicated fans who travel cross-country each weekend in convoys of trailers and motor homes to worship at the concrete shrines of Talladega, Dover, Indianapolis and Martinsville, spending millions of dollars a year on T-shirts, race caps, flags and banners all carrying the logos and car numbers of their favorite drivers.

With their movie-star good looks, drivers such as four-time Nextel Cup champion and Tom Cruise look-alike Jeff Gordon; the blond, surfer-dude cool Jamie McMurray; back-flipper extraordinaire Carl Edwards with his tall, handsome aw-shucks persona; 2005's Nextel Cup runner-up, animal lover and owner of the most piercing blue-green eyes, Greg Biffle; and the 22-year-old red-headed NASCAR wunderkind and TV personality Brian Vickers keep the ladies cheering, screaming and standing in line for hours just for a photo or personal autograph.

Canada's own six-foot-something blond Michael Gold could be Prince William's twin brother and is the darling of CASCAR. The Canadian sport has not been favored with as much media coverage as the big boys down south. However, if sponsors step up to the plate and get behind the drivers racing the Eastern and Western Canadian circuits, there is no end to the fun and excitement that Canadians could enjoy without the need for passports and long drives down through the U.S.

And there are some great up-and-comers from the Busch series (NASCAR's equivalent to baseball's AAA) to watch in 2006, such as Martin Truex Jr.

and Denny Hamlin. These new drivers picked up some Nextel rides during the 2005 season and are primed for full-time campaigns in 2006.

The 2005 race season saw a marked growth in NASCAR audiences, both live at the races and at-home TV viewers. The Daytona 500 in February 2006 even delivered better viewing numbers than the Superbowl. Sponsors have increased their commitments and upped prize winnings, and the celebrity appeal has blossomed with everyone including Ashton Kutcher, The Rock, David Spade, Rob Schneider, James Caan and Pamela Anderson all turning out to make that famous call: "Gentlemen, start your engines." Once Hollywood finds a new idol, the rest of the world soon follows, and this year stock car racing welcomed movie stars, TV, recording and sports celebrities to the tracks, resulting in mainstream news coverage and creating a new breed of heartthrobs and heroes. Even trackside romance novels are now being written to keep up with demand from the ever-growing legions of female fans. These are the new rock-gods on wheels. And boy, are they hot!

Chapter One

Dale Earnhardt Jr.

DATE OF BIRTH: October 10, 1974
BIRTHPLACE: Kannapolis, North Carolina
RESIDES: Mooresville, North Carolina
DRIVES: No. 8 Budweiser Chevrolet

"Junior," or "Little E." as he is known to fans and fellow drivers, is the son of the late NASCAR legend Dale Earnhardt. The famous name he carries has helped boost his media presence, and after he expressed an interest in pursuing an acting career, Madison Avenue came calling a few years ago. Junior has appeared in print advertisements for Drakkar Noir cologne, which is also one of his car sponsors. He also had a role in the video for Sheryl Crow's song "Steve McQueen," which pays homage to the late King of Cool film star famous for his car chase scenes. (Ask any race fan what the greatest car chase scene is and the answer is usually the classic film *Bullitt*, in which McQueen does the majority of his own driving in a dark green Mustang.) Junior starred in several commercials for Wrangler jeans, including one that features

Crow's song. Incidentally, Wrangler was the initial sponsor of his father's No. 3 Chevrolet from 1980 to 1987. Little E. has also done TV ads for Budweiser, NAPA, Domino's Pizza and the somewhat irritating Enterprise Rent-A-Car commercial ("Dale Jr., you best get that door…").

He may not have an Oscar in his immediate future, but he certainly is one of the sport's major pin-up boys. His youthful good looks, Southern charm and that wicked glint in his eye keep the ladies thinking they can tame this bad boy, but Junior has concentrated his passions on the track. He is not only a driver but also a team co-owner (DEI) and owner of his own team (JR Motor-sports). Most recently, he became the host of his own TV show, *Back in the Day*, which features great stories and TV film footage of historic races and stock car racing stars from the '70s and '80s.

At age 17, Junior started his own professional driving career in the street stock division in North Carolina. His first race car was a 1978 Monte Carlo he co-owned with his older brother Kerry, and within two seasons, Little E. had sharpened his driving abilities enough to enter the late-model stock car division. There, he developed an in-depth knowledge of car preparation and chassis setups and competed successfully against Kerry and their sister Kelley. Junior won back-to-back NASCAR Busch Series Championships in 1998 and 1999. With his father's help and guidance, his experience on the Carolina short tracks paid off, and Junior took a giant leap of faith and entered the arena of Winston Cup racing.

The 2000 season was Earnhardt's rookie year in the big leagues, and he did his family name proud. But Matt Kenseth (now driving the DeWalt No. 17) out-raced, out-drove and outshone Junior, taking the Rookie of the Year title away from him with a 42-point winning margin. Still, Junior scored big wins at Texas and Richmond and went on to become the first rookie ever to win the all-star exhibition race. Both the media and race fans sat up and took notice that he was a contender.

Junior also helped recreate a Winston Cup milestone in the 2000 season when he raced alongside his father and brother Kerry in the Michigan International Speedway Pepsi 400. That was only the second time that a father had raced against two sons, the first time being when Lee, Richard and Maurice Petty previously shared the track.

The next year proved to be one of the most exciting yet most tragic seasons that Junior has ever experienced. He started the 2001 season thinking he would suffer the same "sophomore slump" of many rookies, but that year was certainly one for the history books.

At the final turn of the last lap of the Daytona 500, Dale Earnhardt Sr. crashed, and as Junior raced across the finish line seconds later to take second place, his father died on impact with the wall.

The next weekend, Junior raced at Rockingham but crashed on the first lap and retired from the race in 43rd place. But the victories came back, with Little E. taking the checkered flag at Dover and Talladega and then taking the win in an emotionally charged return to Daytona. Junior finished eighth in championship points for the year but first in the hearts of race fans. He had paid the greatest tribute possible to his dad by continuing his race for the Cup in the hope of adding yet another trophy to the Earnhardt family mantelpiece.

Unfortunately, 2002 was not a particularly good year for Junior. He suffered a concussion at the Fontana race in April, but he did not admit to his injury until close to the end of the season. He subsequently failed to place anywhere near the top 10 in the three races following Fontana, finishing no better than 30th. But he did manage to bring home two wins at Talladega, a pair of Bud Pole Awards and an 11th-place finish in the championship standings.

The following year, Junior became a serious title contender, scoring a record-breaking fourth consecutive win at Talladega, but even the loyal fans were beginning to think that he could only win at restrictor plate tracks—his last win on a non-plate track was at Dover in 2001. But Junior buried that doubt when he scored a victory at Phoenix late in the season and notched up a career-best third place in the championship point standings. The

2003 season also marked his first win of the NMPA Most Popular Driver Award.

But 2004 brought another traumatic season for Dale Earnhardt Jr. It started out well when he won the Daytona 500, six years to the day after Dale Sr. scored his only win at the "Great American Race." But on a July weekend off from racing, he crashed the Corvette he was testing for an American LeMans Series race in Sonoma, California, and the car burst into flames with Earnhardt still inside. He suffered second- and third-degree burns on his neck, chin, and legs, and his injuries prevented him from driving two races. He was replaced in the driver's seat in the middle of the season by Martin Truex Jr. (driver for Chance 2 Motorsports, which Junior co-owns with stepmother Teresa Earnhardt) and his DEI teammate John Andretti. But Junior bounced back for Bristol in the fall and became the first driver to win both the Busch race and the Cup race in the same weekend.

Junior managed to qualify for the 10-race Cup chase, and his fifth Nextel Cup win of the season, a career high, was also his fifth win at Talladega. But after Junior uttered an obscenity during the television broadcast, he was penalized 25 points for his violation of a NASCAR rule prohibiting use of obscene language. That, along with two consecutive DNFs in the final 10 races dropped him out of contention, and he eventually finished fifth in the 2004 Nextel Cup chase despite his career-high six wins at Daytona, Atlanta, Richmond, Bristol, Talladega and Phoenix. But on a positive note, Junior also picked up his second consecutive Most Popular Driver Award.

And Junior wins even more as a car owner than he does on the track. Martin Truex Jr. charged late in the 2004 Busch Series season, securing the series championship at Darlington with a strong finish and giving Earnhardt wins for both the driver's championship (1998 and 1999) and the owner's championship (2004) in the NASCAR Busch series. It was a feat he repeated in 2005 with six wins and another owner's championship. Junior also won a lion's share of races as the driver-owner, winning six Busch races in only eight starts from 2002 through 2004. His JR Motorsports also fielded a car in the 2005 USAR Hooters ProCup Series, winning once and qualifying for the Four Champions playoff.

As 2004 drew to a close, there were lots of crew and management changes in the DEI garage, and the 2005 season saw Junior score only one win at Chicagoland in July. Engine failure at California Speedway virtually eliminated Little E. from any possible chance for the Nextel Cup championship, but once he reunited with cousin Tony Eury Jr., who took up the position of new crew chief after the fall Richmond weekend, Earnhardt's results improved immediately. Although he had his worst season ever statistically in 2005, scoring only one win and a 19th-place points effort, Junior took home the NMPA Most Popular Driver Award for the third year in a row.

Dale Jr. entered 2006 with renewed energy and focus and increased his media impact by signing on with XM Satellite Radio for a weekly show that debuted in February during Daytona Speedweek. Junior discusses the latest happenings on the stock car racing circuit as well as music, video games and his other personal interests. He also signed on to play a role in various promotions as part of a multi-year agreement with XM. In addition, he created his own production company, Hammerhead Entertainment, to produce his TV show, *Back in the Day*, for Speed Channel. His driver earnings stood at close to $30 million, but revenue from all the additional media initiatives was expected to soon put him in Jeff Gordon territory.

But all work and no play make Dale Jr.—well, pretty happy! But NASCAR's most eligible bachelor seemed to have finally found romance with Emily Maynard, who was originally engaged to the late Ricky Hendrick (who was killed along with other Hendrick Motorsports team members and family in a horrific 2004 helicopter crash). Prior to Emily, he had been linked with several beautiful models and TV personalities, including *Playboy* cover girl Leeann Velez Tweeden earlier in 2005. And in 2000, MTV's *Wannabe a VJ* reality TV show runner-up Shannon Wiseman kept Junior company for a short time after meeting him when he co-hosted a local Charlotte radio show.

But there is another great love in Junior's life—his boxer dog, Killer. Like many of his track buddies, Junior is an animal lover, and he and Killer are featured in Greg Biffle's 2006 calendar of NASCAR drivers and their pets that raised money for humane societies across the U.S. Earnhardt supports many other charities too, especially sick and disabled children's causes.

Junior, or as his father Dale Earnhardt Sr. used to call him, "Junebug," is a third-generation stock car driver who has followed closely in the tire treads of his grandfather, Ralph Earnhardt, and his legendary dad, Dale Earnhardt Sr. It seems as if Little E. has finally stepped out of his famous father's shadow. Dale Earnhardt Jr. is carving out his own niche in stock car racing history and in the hearts of his own fans.

Chapter Two

Jamie McMurray

DATE OF BIRTH: June 3, 1976
BIRTHPLACE: Joplin, Missouri
RESIDES: Charlotte, North Carolina area
DRIVES: No. 26 Sharpie/Crown Royal Ford

Jamie McMurray is, without a doubt, the Brad Pitt of NASCAR. His tousled blond hair and wide toothy smile melt female race fans' hearts at every NASCAR track, yet his steely determination to take the checkered flag keeps him firmly grounded in the boys' club. For some time, his status as the track's number-one bachelor heart-throb was in doubt when he was seriously dating Cielo Garcia, NASCAR's former Miss Winston model. Then, in early 2005, he started a relationship with Katie Wallace, the pretty 20-something daughter of NASCAR legend and Busch Series teammate Rusty Wallace.

It appears he's back on the dating scene, but his love of stock car racing seems to be his number one priority right now. The 2005 season marked Jamie's third year of NASCAR Nextel Cup racing, and he finished just out of the top 10 in a respectable 12th place position, winning close to $4 million. It's not known how much he earned for his brief cameo role in Lindsay Lohan's summer movie, *Herbie Fully Loaded*, but his younger fans certainly loved seeing him on the big screen with other NASCAR stars. He also appeared in *TV Guide*, *USA Weekend* and *Maxim* magazines and made cameo appearances on *The West Wing*, was a guest on MTV *Cribs* and will participate in the FX Network's hit show *NASCAR Drivers: 360*.

In July '05, McMurray signed a contract to drive for Roush Racing starting in the 2007 season. However, trouble came when the media caught wind of the switch and other team changes and career decisions being made by several high-profile drivers. Jamie's hopes for an early release from his contract with Chip Ganassi became public knowledge, and Ganassi was reluctant to oblige. Jamie's situation became more complicated when Kurt Busch decided to leave Roush to drive for Penske Racing in 2007. This would then leave Penske with an empty driver's seat in the No. 2 Dodge in 2006 since Rusty Wallace had retired. They wanted to put Busch in that car right away. Confused yet? It became even more complicated. After Kurt Busch's infamous run-in with the Phoenix sheriff's department with just two races left to go in the championship, Jack Roush dumped Busch, leaving him with two seats to fill: Busch's car as well as the seat McMurray was supposed to fill when Mark Martin retired.

Martin decided to remain in the Roush No. 6 Ford for one last season, so Jamie will drive Kurt's No. 97 car (now renumbered No. 26). Where he will take it in the 2006 Cup chase is still in the future, but the journey Jamie has taken to even reach the starting grid, like many of his comrades on wheels, has been exciting and filled with triumphs as well as a few disappointments.

The young McMurray started racing go-karts in Joplin, Missouri, when he was just eight years old. He spent nearly 10 years racing nationally and internationally, winning four U.S. go-kart titles between 1986 and 1992 and a World Go-Kart Championship in 1991. Jamie's father, Jim, spent every waking hour working with Jamie on the karts, traveling with the young driver to every kart track across the country.

A weekend funny car racer, Jim McMurray took his son along with him to every event. Jamie attended his first race when he was only three weeks old, riding in the truck that towed his dad's funny car back to the pits after each run. When his dad raced, the whole family was there too. The senior McMurray reminisced recently that while he raced around the tracks, his son played with toy cars in the track sandbox with the other drivers' kids.

After his own nearly three decades of racing, Jim quit to focus on his son's unquestionable passion for speed. The World Karting Association holds its annual road racing championships at Daytona International Speedway starting December 26, and young Jamie and his family often spent Christmas in their motor home parked in a shopping center lot. On other occasions, father and son drove down to Daytona on Christmas Day after opening their presents with the rest of the family, but the sacrifice was rewarded when Jamie won a title in 1990.

The father-son bond runs deep in the McMurray family. Although the teen years are often difficult times when young men are testing their boundaries, Jamie maintains he and his father never argued about anything except for racing, probably because they both loved it so much. Jim McMurray could only attend about seven races a year in those early days because his work kept him away from the track. He had to settle for watching Jamie's races on TV, holding his breath at every turn.

Go-karting was fun, but Jamie was looking for something bigger that offered more horsepower. So in 1992, he switched to asphalt modifieds and late models with his dad before moving on to other teams after he turned 20. He became Track Champion at the I-44 Speedway in Lebanon, Missouri, in 1997, defeating the former NASCAR Winston Racing Series champion Larry Phillips for the title.

The following year, Jamie competed in the ARTCO and NASCAR RE/MAX Challenge Series.

In 1999, he made his Craftsman Truck Series debut at I-70 Speedway in Odessa, Missouri, competing in the RE/MAX Challenge Series and five NASCAR Craftsman Truck Series races. Jamie joined the series full time in 2000.

Jamie's career moved into even higher gear in 2000 when he was named to drive the No. 27 Williams TravelCenters car for Brewco Motorsports in the Busch Series Grand National Division, making his debut on October 29 at the Memphis Motorsports Park. He also competed in the Busch Series race at the Phoenix International Raceway on November 4 and continued driving in 15 NASCAR Craftsman Truck Series events. McMurray won Bud Pole Awards at the Michigan Speedway and the Nashville Speedway USA, posting one top-five result and three top-10 finishes with a season-best third-place finish at Indianapolis Raceway Park.

Jamie ran a full Busch Grand National season in 2001, taking the seat vacated by Casey Atwood when he moved to the Winston Cup series to drive for Ray Evernham's Dodge team. He competed in all 33 NASCAR Busch Series events, securing three top-10 finishes, which resulted in a third-place standing for the Raybestos Rookie of the Year and 16th place in the overall Busch Series point standings.

Then came 2002. Jamie turned the racing world on its ear as he scored his first NASCAR Winston Cup victory in only his second start in the series on October 13 in the UAW-GM Quality 500 at Lowe's Motor Speedway in Charlotte, North Carolina. Veteran driver Sterling Marlin had been injured a couple of weeks earlier, and team owner Chip Ganassi had already scouted the talented youth as a possible third driver for 2003 but hadn't even presented him with a contract when he asked Jamie to fill Marlin's seat. Talk about a Cinderella story. As the checkered flag came down after the 500-mile race, Jamie drove straight into Victory Lane. "Jamie showed a lot of heart when I first met him," Ganassi said. "He's got great communication skills, and I think what you see is a genuine person."

McMurray continued through the rest of the season, setting a new NASCAR modern-era record by becoming the quickest driver to win a Winston Cup race. In six Winston Cup starts that year, apart from the Lowe's victory, he posted one top-five, two top-10 and three top-15 finishes. It was a breakout year for Jamie's Busch Series, too. He scored two victories (Atlanta and Rockingham), made six top-five and 14 top-10 finishes and finished sixth in the final Busch Series standings. Jamie was often quoted as saying he owed much of his early success to his then-girlfriend and good-luck charm, Cielo Garcia, a former model and spokesperson for NASCAR who had to relinquish her title in order to date Jamie. (NASCAR rules forbade a Miss Winston from dating a Winston Cup driver.)

NASCAR now had a new star. Jamie was subsequently named driver of Chip Ganassi Racing's No. 42 Havoline Dodge for the 2003 NASCAR Winston Cup Series. Activity on the various fan websites suddenly started listing the name Jamie McMurray alongside that other favorite track hottie, Jeff Gordon.

The 2003 NASCAR Raybestos Winston Cup Rookie of the Year title soon followed as Jamie competed in all 36 Winston Cup races that year, scoring five top-five and 13 top-10 finishes plus taking one Bud Pole Award. He finished a lucky 13th in the final 2003 NASCAR Winston Cup Series point standings. Always the multi-tasker, he also drove in 19 NASCAR Busch Series races that same season, finishing with two wins, six top-fives and nine top-10s.

The 2004 Nextel Cup season marked Jamie's sophomore year for the Ganassi team, posting nine top-five and 23 top-10 finishes en route to finishing 11th in points and picking up a million-dollar bonus plus a trip to New York to the end-of-season championship dinner. He also scored three Busch Series victories with three different teams during the season and tied a NASCAR record by winning his fourth consecutive Busch Series victory at North Carolina Speedway.

He closed out the 2005 season 12th in the standings with one pole, four top-five finishes and 10 top-10 results. With so many of NASCAR's elder statesmen retiring (Rusty, Ricky Rudd, then Mark Martin after the '06 season), the top of the rankings list looks ripe for Jamie to move on up.

Even with all the hard work behind the wheel, Jamie knows he owes much of his success and popularity to the support of his fans who stand in line for hours waiting for photo ops and autographs. But it was his number one fan, his dad, who was lucky enough to be at Charlotte, North Carolina, sharing that exciting fall afternoon when Jamie won the 2002 Winston Cup Lowe's Motor Speedway race. Jamie won't forget having him there and taking the Victory Lane photos with his dad and the team. The proud father stands in the front row, holding up the number one finger.

Chapter Three

J.J. Yeley
(Born Christopher Beltram Hernandez Yeley)

DATE OF BIRTH: October 5, 1976

BIRTHPLACE: Phoenix, Arizona

RESIDES: Indianapolis, Indiana
(relocating to Charlotte, North Carolina)

DRIVES: No.18 Interstate Batteries Chevrolet
(Nextel Cup series), No.18 Home Depot/Vigoro
Chevrolet (Busch Series)

The son of "Cactus" Jack Yeley (the seven-time Arizona Midget Racing Association champion and two-time World of Outlaws Midget champion), young Christopher "J.J." Yeley was truly born to race.

By age 10, he was strapped in behind the wheel of a quarter-midget go-kart, and by 14, he was racing full midgets in the Arizona Midget Racing Association, just as his father had done before him. In 1991, J.J. won the series' Rookie of the Year title. By age 17, he was in a non-wing sprint car setting track records. Yeley took the Hoosier state by storm during 1997's Indiana Sprintweek, winning the series and capturing the USAC National Sprint Car Series Rookie of the Year Award, despite starting only some of the races in the series.

J.J. continued scoring open-wheel successes, starting four races in the Indy Racing League Indy Car Series with one top-10 finish to his credit. This allowed him to compete at the famed Indianapolis Motor Speedway in 1998, becoming the youngest driver (at age 21) to qualify for the race, which was celebrating its 82nd year of running. J.J. posted the 13th-fastest qualifying time with an average speed of 218 miles per hour, making him the fastest qualifying rookie. He managed to stay out of trouble throughout the race, although he nearly spun out eventual race winner Eddie Cheever Jr. The young driver finished a respectable ninth. He has frequently stated that the race was one of his career highlights. Following the Indy 500, J.J. completed in five Pep Boys Indy Racing League events.

Yeley returned to the Indy Racing League in 2000 with McCormack Motorsports, but after struggling with a lack of funding and less success on the track, he eventually returned to the USAC racing family. J.J. picked up right where he left off. By 2001, he was getting to be well known around the tracks, and media and fans were discovering this handsome young man behind the wheel. He claimed that season's USAC Sprint Car Championship, finished third in the midget standings and fourth in the Silver Crown, and he was the only driver to finish in the top five in all series. He not only won that year, but he also took the 2003 National Sprint, the 2002 and 2003 Silver Crown and the 2003 National Midget Series titles.

When he picked up the championship in all three of USAC's top divisions, J.J. became only the second driver to ever accomplish the feat. Current Nextel champ Tony Stewart was the first to pull off the "Triple Crown" in 1995. Coincidentally, Stewart owned the sprint and Silver Crown cars Yeley drove to win the championship. And the Tony connection continued as the midget car J.J. piloted that year was the same car (with the same owner) Stewart drove to win the midget title in his "Triple Crown" year.

But the youngster dominated his season and improved on Stewart's star-making performance by claiming the Triple Crown after completing an incredible season. J.J. scored 24 USAC feature victories to set a new single-season record, becoming the only driver ever to win on pavement and dirt in all three national series in a single year. When he eventually moved to NASCAR, he had already secured 51 career USAC wins and a total of five USAC championships since 1997. When he got the call up to the big leagues in 2004, J.J. signed to the same team as Stewart—Joe Gibbs Racing. The team gave him his first career opportunity to qualify for a Nextel Cup event in 2005 when Stewart was injured.

Yeley started in NASCAR by competing in 17 Busch Series events in the Joe Gibbs No. 18 Home Depot/Vigoro Chevrolet. In his first season, J.J. produced four top-10 finishes, including a career best finish of sixth at Kansas Speedway. He also made his debut in the Nextel Cup Series in 2004 by qualifying for the Pop Secret 300 at California Speedway.

Going into the 2005 season, J.J continued to drive the No. 18 Vigoro Chevrolet for a full season of the Busch Series and finished the season 11th in the points standings. He also drove the No. 11 FedEx Nextel Cup car for four races, giving him valuable track and racing experience in the Nextel Cup car.

For the 2006 Nextel season, the 30-year-old driver will compete for Rookie of the Year honors along with fellow JGR teammate Denny Hamlin. He will also pull double duty by driving a second full season in the Busch Series.

But J.J. still finds time in his hectic race schedule to take in some golf, and he also enjoys spending time on his boat with wife Kristen and their new daughter, Faith (born in May 2005).

Chapter Four

Kurt Busch

DATE OF BIRTH: August 4, 1978

BIRTHPLACE: Las Vegas, Nevada

RESIDES: Concord, North Carolina

DRIVES: No. 2 Miller Lite Dodge

Tom and Gaye Busch knew early on that they had a racing wunderkind on their hands in their first-born son, Kurt. In fact, they would soon learn that their second son, Kyle, was also pretty handy behind the wheel, but Kurt was the first one out on the track.

Born in the late '70s, long after Elvis had left the building (and the planet), Kurt Busch learned everything he could about cars and racing from his dad, himself a second-generation racer and auto mechanic. The eager youngster was racing cars long before he was permitted to drive a street-legal car, and papa Busch introduced Kurt to the dwarf car series when he was just 14 years old. At age 15, Kurt had already made a name for himself in his hometown of Las Vegas driving the family-owned dwarf series car at a half-mile clay track outside Las Vegas known as Pahrump Valley Speedway. By 16, he had been named Nevada's Rookie of the Year, and he became series champion one year later. In 1996, he won the hobby stock championship at the Bullring at Las Vegas Speedway Park, quickly gaining the attention of several owners in the various NASCAR regional touring series.

Going into 1997, Busch kept busy racing late models, American race trucks, Legend cars and dwarf cars but left for a period to attend college at the University of Arizona. He thought about a more dependable career as a pharmacist, but Kurt was soon back home at the track in Las Vegas with his mind focused and ready to pursue a career in racing.

That same year, he started competing in the NASCAR Southwest Touring series, and his early successes garnered him Rookie of the Year honors in 1998 after he posted three top-five and seven top-10 finishes in 17 starts. He also kept himself busy by scoring 15 wins in the Legends cars and American modified series.

As the 1999 racing season progressed, Kurt took six wins in the Southwest Touring series and was awarded the Southwest Touring Championship. He also posted a top-10 finish in his first Winston West race, finishing in eighth at Las Vegas Motor Speedway in front of a hometown crowd. At Jack Roush's infamous "Gong Show" talent showcase that year, Kurt earned himself the chance to drive in the rough-and-tumble Craftsman Truck Series, eventually signing a multi-year contract to drive for Roush Racing beginning in the year 2000.

Ringing in the new millennium, Kurt's first season competing in the trucks netted him four poles and four wins—a no-brainer for 2000's Rookie of the Year honors! He even managed to finish second in the overall series standings, tying teammate and future truck champ Greg Biffle with four pole awards. Busch's spectacular debut in the Truck Series, coupled with his innate ability to adapt to new cars, inspired Jack Roush to promote Busch directly to behind the wheel of a Winston Cup car. In doing so, Kurt bypassed the traditional gradual journey through the Busch series that is the normal career progression, which allows a young driver to gain stock car racing experience and track savvy. Kurt Busch competed in seven Winston Cup races in 2000, doing well but with a best finish of just 13th at Lowe's Motor Speedway.

But Roush's unprecedented gamble with Kurt Busch paid off big in 2001. Kurt won his first career Winston Cup pole at Darlington and posted six top-10 finishes, and although he finished 27th in the overall standings, he was runner-up for the Raybestos Rookie of the Year title, just losing out to Kevin Harvick. By the end of the season, Roush gambled again, this time swapping Busch's crew with teammate Mark Martin's. Roush paired

Busch with veteran crew chief Jimmy Fennig, and they just clicked.

In 2002, Martin and Busch finished second and third respectively in the Winston Cup standings, with Kurt scoring his first career Winston Cup win at Bristol Motor Speedway early in the season. He notched up three more victories (Martinsville, Atlanta, and Homestead) and finished out the season with 12 top-five and 21 top-10 results.

Kurt suffered a roller-coaster ride throughout 2003, earning four wins, nine top-five and 14 top-10 results. He had four second-place finishes, including a .002-second loss to Ricky Craven at Darlington, the closest margin of victory in the sport since the advent of electronic timing and scoring. As the two cars crossed the finish line, the space between their two bumpers was so small that it was as if they were glued together. Yet despite all the effort, Kurt finished a disappointing 11th in the Cup standings. His pain was eased, however, with more than $5 million as his big end-of-season paycheck. He also pulled double-duty in the IROC series and won the championship with one victory and finishes of fourth place or better in all four events.

But Busch's reputation as a driver and as a fair sportsman took a beating when an ongoing feud with fellow driver Jimmy Spencer (now a regular TV contributor for the Speed Network) turned violent. After some aggressive bumping throughout the Michigan International Speedway Cup race, Spencer hit Busch's vehicle with his car after the checkered flag had dropped and then walked over to Kurt's car and punched him. Both drivers received hefty fines and were placed on probation for the rest of the year. The on- and off-track altercations significantly dampened race fans' fondness for Kurt. His reputation for bad behavior, public displays of aggression and (as many consider it) pomposity has made Kurt one of the sport's least-popular personalities, even though he went on to capture the Nextel Cup championship crown in brilliant driving style.

And that championship wasn't long in coming! In 2004, Kurt had three wins, including his third consecutive win at Bristol and a sweep of both races at Loudon. He also led 746 laps over 21 events and held on to win the tightest points race in NASCAR history, with an eight-point margin over Jimmie Johnson in second place.

The championship title also brought newfound celebrity and even greater wealth to Kurt. He collected a $5.3 million prize purse for winning the championship, bringing his career winnings total to $22.8 million. The champ worked the talk show circuit, had photo shoots with President George W. Bush and attended and supported numerous charity events. But his on-track aggression didn't diminish, and again he was penalized by race officials and booed by fans at the tracks.

What started out as a promising 2005 season was cut short near the end of the Chase for the Cup when Kurt and long-time girlfriend (now fiancée) Eva Bryan had a run-in with Maricopa County Sheriff deputies, who had pulled Kurt's vehicle over for suspicion of drunk driving. In a scene right out of the Oscar-winning film *Crash*, Eva apparently had plenty to say and created a tense scene by arguing with the deputy. She stated that it was her fault Kurt had been driving erratically because of an ongoing family disagreement. Eventually Kurt's father, Tom, was called, and he arrived to take over the controls of the car. After various tests and a few days of media speculation, accusation and denials, the incident ended with an inconclusive blood alcohol reading and some bad publicity for the Sheriff's office about similar incidents "targeting" race car drivers and celebrities in that particular county. However, Kurt was unceremoniously suspended by the Roush Racing organization, which offered little support for the driver during the week of media scrutiny and unfounded rumors of drunk driving.

Kurt had already tried to negotiate an early released from his driving contract with Jack Roush so he could move over to Roger Penske's organization, taking over the No. 2 Miller Lite Dodge Charger seat vacated by the retiring Rusty Wallace. Jack Roush had sternly refused, but this incident gave Roush Racing an out and ultimately gave Kurt an in. Roush tore up the contract, and Busch and Penske sat down with pens in hand and inked a new driver contract for 2006. In turn, Chip Ganassi released Jamie McMurray from his contract with the No. 42 car, and Jamie slipped into the Roush garage to replace Kurt. All in all, not a bad outcome for a touchy situation.

Kurt had met Eva Bryan on a blind date in July 2003 set up by a friend who told Eva that Kurt was a veterinarian. Kurt suggested that such a lovely lady wouldn't want to meet a redneck stock car driver, so for that post-race Sunday night, he became a pet doctor. He later found out that Eva wasn't at all put off by his true profession, and she has spent almost every Sunday afternoon since that night sitting in her beau's pit and watching him race. She also enjoys sharing the couch with him in their infield trailer during race season watching Kurt's favorite ball team, the Chicago Cubs.

Kurt eventually proposed to Eva during the last off-week of 2005's Nextel Cup season while the couple was taking a quick vacation in Prague to watch the Hungarian Grand Prix Formula One race. The pair planned a wedding in the summer of 2006, and there is every possibility that their beloved terrier, Jim, might be the ring bearer.

During the Texas Motor Speedway race in April 2006, Busch wrecked Greg Biffle, who had led the race for 49 laps. He got the nose of his No. 2 under Biffle's rear bumper, causing him to spin out and crash against both the outside and inside barriers.

The maneuver was an obvious infraction that took Biffle out of the race and further out of Cup contention. Biffle's girlfriend, Nicole Lunders, took it badly, first slamming a water bottle against the side of the pit box and then marching over to Kurt's pit box, mounting the stairs and having heated words with Eva Bryan. On-track cameras caught all the action—as did race officials who subsequently called both women into the front office for some disciplinary discussions.

The media had a field day with the apparent "cat fight." However, both women had previously been good friends, and before the end of the race, they text-messaged each other to apologize, with Nicole expressing remorse over her emotional outburst. After the race, Kurt refused to take any personal blame, and Biffle had few words to say on the matter, but his disappointment was evident. Unlike the stoic driver, racing officials, media and the fans have made their feelings about Kurt Busch known very loudly.

Chapter Five

Jeremy Mayfield

DATE OF BIRTH: May 27, 1969
BIRTHPLACE: Owensboro, Kentucky
RESIDES: Mooresville, North Carolina
DRIVES: No. 19 Dodge Dealers/UAW Dodge

Jeremy Mayfield was one little boy who couldn't wait to get to grandma's house. At age four, he had created a racing oval in his grandmother's back garden in Owensboro, Kentucky, and spent hours racing his kiddie motorcycle around and around. Even at this young age, Jeremy proved he had a passion for speed. His backyard laps were excellent training for his first job, an early morning paper route that young Jeremy covered quickly, starting around 5:00 AM and pedaling his bike through the neighborhood.

By age 10, he had graduated to racing BMX bikes at the local track and soon began racing go-karts three or four nights a week after school. The go-karts led to street-stock racing at Kentucky Motor Speedway, where he was so successful that race officials impounded his car because he had too many wins (a rule in this division). But the frustration didn't dampen his spirits, and he soon moved on to late-model racing. Jeremy made frequent visits to Nashville to compete, and not only did he race, but in order to finance all the expenses involved, he also painted the signs along the track and the numbers on the race cars.

At age 19, Jeremy made a permanent move to Nashville, where he worked as a fabricator at Sadler Racing. He was determined to take up racing full time, and his wishes were granted six months later when the Sadlers gave him a late-model car to race.

In 1987, Jeremy moved to the ARCA Series, where he finished the season with eight top-five and 10 top-10 finishes as well as taking Rookie of the Year honors from Kentucky Motor Speedway. Drivers and team owners in the Cup community also began to notice him.

But it took a few more years and several thousand racing miles before he made his debut in a Cup car. On October 10, 1993, at Charlotte Motor Speedway, Jeremy finished 10 laps down in 29th. A few years later, the legendary Carl Yarborough offered him a ride, and Jeremy made the commitment to full-time Cup racing. That year, Jeremy finished 31st in points with one top-10 finish in 27 starts.

Mayfield notched his first career pole at Talladega in 1996 and earned a pair of top-five finishes, but the wins just weren't there. Late in the '96 season, Yarborough released Jeremy from his contract, swapping drivers with owner Michael Kranefuss. John Andretti took over from Jeremy.

For the next two years, Jeremy enjoyed some success with Kranefuss, earning his first career win in the Pocono 500 and his best points finish to date in 1998 with a seventh-place standing. After Kranefuss joined forces with Roger Penske, Jeremy hit his stride and started scoring wins and poles.

However, things started unraveling for the team when Mayfield's car was found to be too low after his win at California in 2000. Although this had nothing to do with Jeremy, the chemistry fizzled out. The nail in the coffin was hammered down when race officials found additive in the car's gas tank just before Jeremy's pole-position run at Talladega. Everyone was ready for a change, and Jeremy needed to break away from the negativity surrounding his current team.

So, in September 2001, he was released from his contract and spent the following five months looking for his next ride. Just as Speedweek 2002 started, Evernham Motorsports came knocking, and Jeremy found himself behind the wheel of the No. 19 Dodge Dealers/UAW Dodge.

Although Mayfield had the expertise and might of Evernham's great racing organization behind him, the wins still weren't coming. During the 2003 season, Jeremy didn't score a single first-place result, and he managed only a few second-place finishes towards the end of the season. However, the 2004 and 2005 seasons proved his worth as he finished 10th and then ninth in the Cup point standings.

For the 2004 season, Jeremy just squeaked in to the top 10 for the Cup Chase, thanks to a dominant performance at Richmond in the 26th and final race that allowed drivers to earn a berth in the inaugural Chase field. He took the win, and by leading the most laps, he collected every point available. The race gave him enough points to secure his 10th-place position in the Chase field. Unfortunately, the No. 19 was caught up in an accident in the first Chase race, resulting in a points setback that was just too much for the team to overcome. Still, the 10th-place final finish was a good springboard for the upcoming season and an opportunity to rebuild team motivation and commitment.

Jeremy Mayfield joined an elite group of Nextel Cup Series drivers in 2005 when he claimed his place in the Chase for the Cup field for the second consecutive year—one of only seven Nextel Cup drivers to accomplish the feat. His win at Michigan in August secured his top-10 eligibility with only three races remaining before the Chase field was set. When the 10-race shootout started, he stood seventh in the point standings and had the distinction of completing more laps than any other driver. Jeremy was still in contention halfway through the Chase, trailing the leader by only 115 points, but the No. 19 team's efforts fell short, and they had to settle for a ninth-place finish in the final standings. With a win at Michigan, Jeremy also had four top-five and nine top-10 finishes in the '05 season, a record most other teams would be pleased to hold.

Going into the 2006 season, a number of challenges face the No. 19 team. First, they want to make the Chase field for a third consecutive time, a difficult and record-setting feat. If that wish is fulfilled, they then need to eliminate the problems that have plagued the team and find a formula to take them to the Cup's Victory Lane.

Team owner Ray Evernham started putting all the components in place before the final race of 2005, introducing a revolutionary new structure for all Evernham Motorsports teams that was designed to foster better collective thinking, decision making and intellectual innovation. The program eliminated the position of crew chief by replacing it with a leadership group made up of a team director, a car director and an engineer. Jeremy started out the 2006 season with Chris Andrews as his team director, Kirk Almquist as his car director and Tim Malinovsky as the engineer. Time will tell if this structure will bring the wins to Evernham's drivers and create a new formula that other teams may emulate or adapt.

Away from the racetrack, the handsome six-footer and his wife, Shana, like to relax by living the simple life—just throw a few action movies into the DVD player, and they're happy. They also enjoy taking off and just spending quiet time together.

The Mayfields also support several charities, including fellow racer Kyle Petty's Victory Junction Gang Camp, The Leukemia and Lymphoma Society, Motor Racing Outreach, the American Cancer Society and the Pug Rescue of North Carolina. Shana and Jeremy are proud owners of Mattie, a cute pug who accompanies them to all the races.

Chapter Six

Greg Biffle

DATE OF BIRTH: December 23, 1969

BIRTHPLACE: Vancouver, Washington

RESIDES: Mooresville, North Carolina

DRIVES: No. 16 National Guard/Subway Ford (Nextel Series), No. 16 AmeriQuest Ford (Busch Series)

For many fans, 2005 belonged to Greg Biffle. He may not have won the championship, placing second and missing first place title by only 35 points, but race after race, he won many new fans, especially those of the female persuasion, with his courageous driving, classy post-race interviews and his selfless commitment to the smallest victims of Hurricane Katrina—the animals.

The 5'10", blue-eyed 36-year-old driver of the National Guard No. 16 Ford was one of the first to answer the call when Hurricane Katrina blew New Orleans away and left not only the people but also their pets stranded without help or hope. Along with fellow speed demon Ryan Newman and his wife Krissie, Biffle and girlfriend Nicole Lunders raised awareness and funding for animal rescue operations, helping save the lives of hundreds of family pets. His love of animals and support for no-kill shelters has endeared "Biff" (as he's known trackside) to legions of predominantly female fans who appreciate his softer side.

The ultimate multi-tasker, in 2005, Biffle drove in all 36 Nextel Cup races, scoring six victories as well as 15 top-five and 21 top-ten results on his way to a second-place finish in the 2005 championship standings. His season concluded with one of the most exciting, nail-biting drives to the checkered flag ever witnessed. There was barely a wheel well's difference between Biffle's winning result and veteran Mark Martin's second-place finish as the cars crossed the line at Homestead-Miami. Although Tony Stewart's finish way back in the pack still assured him of his championship, Biffle enjoyed the end-of-season triumph with a noisy burnout in front of thousands of fans in the stands. The 2002 Busch Series champion, Biffle also drove in a partial schedule of 27 races in the '05 Busch Series, scoring one win, 16 top-five and 21 top-10 results on his way to a 10th-place finish in the championship, just one point behind the ninth-place position. Half of his top-five finishes, eight in total, were second-place results. One can only imagine what Biffle could have accomplished had he run the entire 35-race Busch schedule.

Nonetheless, he ran an amazing Cup season that brought him to within 35 points of the Nextel championship. In a post-race news conference, he said, "I'm excited about the win, thankful for all the opportunities I've gotten this season, that Doug [Richert, crew chief] and Jack [Roush, team owner] have given me my entire career and then to come off this season with six wins and be second in points, only 35 back behind a two-time champion like Tony Stewart. I can't think of a way to finish this season out any better."

Armed with an engineering degree, Biffle is as comfortable under a car as he is inside one. His knowledge and experience allow him to work closely with his crew chief, and throughout each race, he analyzes every little noise, vibration and engine aberration, which helps his pit crew to make the necessary adjustments—although not always successfully. Don't ever mention lug nuts to Biff. Had it not been for a loose wheel at Texas after a crew error with lug nuts, a flat tire at Dover and a poor showing at Talladega, Greg Biffle would have become the first driver in history to claim championships in the top three levels of NASCAR competition—Nextel Cup, Busch and Craftsman Truck series—not to mention his 2001 NBS Rookie of the Year and 1998 NCTS Rookie of the Year honors.

But it's taken Greg Biffle a decade of hard work and commitment to come this close to tasting the ultimate victory spoils. His father bought him his first car at age 15—a 1976 Firebird. At 17, he tore around oval tracks in Washington State in his first stock car, a 1972 Ford Torino. Encouraged by his father and his own growing confidence, he eventually came up through NASCAR's Weekly Racing Series. The weekly races honed his skills, and he learned to balance his natural aggressiveness with good car control, recording notable statistics in other series including the NASCAR Winston Racing Series championships at Portland Speedway and the Tri-Cities Raceway.

Former NASCAR Hall of Fame champion and broadcaster Benny Parsons first recommended Jack Roush check out the fresh new driver. During the 1995–96 NASCAR Winter Heat Series, Biffle caught Parson's attention. The young man's tenacity and focus impressed the retired racer. By 1997, Biffle had successfully competed in one of NASCAR's regional touring series when a friend passed along the news that team owner Jack Roush was interested and wanted to discuss a contract.

Biffle, then 28, had to go to Charlotte, North Carolina, to negotiate. So without any hesitation, he closed up his business in Vancouver, where he ran a race car shop and café, and headed east to make a deal with Jack Roush that would catapult him into racing stardom. The advance buzz on Biffle was so hot that although neither Roush nor Geoff Smith (president of Roush Racing) had met him in person, a contract was already on the table when Biff arrived.

His success with Roush Racing seemed to come almost instantly. Biffle won 1998's Rookie of the Year honors in the Craftsman Truck Series, also establishing a rookie record for Bud Pole positions (four). Adding to that success, he was the series runner-up in 1999 and then won the championship in 2000. Roush promoted Biffle to the Busch Series in 2001, where he again became top rookie, driving the Grainger Ford Taurus like a seasoned veteran. In his 33 races driven, he scored five wins, two poles, 16 top-five finishes and 21 top-10 results. Biffle's team set eight rookie records, including most wins, most top-five finishes, most top-10 finishes, most starts, most points overall (4509), most laps led (948), most races led (19) and most money won. He followed that success with the Busch championship title in 2002, becoming the first driver to win over $2 million in a single Busch Series season.

During this time, Greg met girlfriend Nicole Lunders, who has worked with him to establish the Greg Biffle Foundation. The organization builds awareness and serves as an advocate to improve the well-being of animals by harnessing the power and passion of the motor sports industry. Nicole travels with Biff for most of the racing season and has started several fundraising projects for the foundation. They also share the love and devotion of two boxer dogs, Gracie and Foster.

An avid angler, Biffle has become an expert bass fisherman and competed in several celebrity pro-am tournaments. He got hooked a few years ago and appreciates the similarities between the two sports and between fishermen and NASCAR fans. And the angling world appreciates him. In fact, the Bass Anglers Sportsman Society (BASS), which operates the world championship of bass fishing, the Classic, has become an associate sponsor of the No. 16 car.

He's also a keen pilot and often flies his private jet from city to city throughout the racing season. Off-season, he enjoys racing recreational off-road vehicles with fellow NASCAR driver and friend Robby Gordon.

But even with all these perks and fancy toys, he remains a self-described "regular guy" who just loves to go fast. In a sport that has become increasingly overrun with star personalities and where off-track activities seem more important than the race itself, Biffle avoids all the fuss and commotion of celebrity. His attitude has endeared him to old-school fans and industry types, who see him as a throw back to drivers of the '70s and '80s. Although he's as much of a fun guy as the next, he remains professional and conservative around the track—which is how both the sponsors and the NASCAR organization like their drivers.

Biffle has often been described as a wheelman, which in racing terminology is quite a compliment. A wheelman drives with the finesse of a surgeon, delicately threading his car through traffic. He drives cleanly, but he's not above the occasional bump-draft to push ahead of the field. A wheelman not only drives smart, but also drives as if each lap is the race to the checkered flag.

Respect for Biffle comes easily to his pit crew. Each week, the Busch Series team dry-cleans all his seat covers to ensure a fresh, clean-smelling interior. As one veteran crewmember once explained, "Everybody here has just got so much respect for him. He makes you want to do that for him."

Greg Biffle is not only a great driver, but he also possesses an easy-going personality and is fun to be around. The fans love him for it, and his humility and willingness to help those less fortunate elevate him beyond mere heartthrob status. He's the real deal.

Chapter Seven

Casey Mears

DATE OF BIRTH: March 12, 1978
BIRTHPLACE: Bakersfield, California
RESIDES: Huntersville, North Carolina
DRIVES: No. 42 Texaco/Havoline Dodge

If ever there was a driver who had "racing in the blood," it has be Casey Mears, who grew up in a family heavily involved in open-wheel racing. His father, Roger, competed in Indy cars for several years, but his real passion was off-road racing. Casey's Uncle Rick is known as one of the greatest open-wheel drivers of all time and is a four-time winner of the Indianapolis 500.

Casey thought he would continue to follow his family's footsteps and pursue an open-wheel racing career. But his destiny was set in November 2001 when he decided to move to the NASCAR Busch Series Grand National division as driver of the No. 66 Phillips Dodge for Welliver-Jesel Motorsports.

His parents and family were supportive of the young race car driver's decision to move from the CART Series to stock cars. NASCAR is currently considered the most popular form of motorsports in North America, and every driver wants to compete at the highest level possible.

Casey Mears was born on March 12, 1978, in Bakersfield, California, and started racing before he even started school. At age four, he was racing BMX bicycles, and by six, he was competing in ATVs at Bakersfield Speedway. He continued racing ATVs before moving to go-karts in 1991, spending one full season racing karts before moving on to the SuperLites Off-Road Series in 1992, where he recorded several top-three finishes.

Casey then moved on to the Jim Russell USAC Triple Crown in 1994, scoring a victory at Mesa Marin Raceway and finishing an impressive third in the series standings. In 1995, Casey scored the Jim Russell USAC Triple Crown championship. He made his Indy Lights debut in 1996 at the Cleveland Grand Prix, finishing eighth. By 1997, Casey was competing full time in the Indy Lights series and looking to challenge for a championship.

Although they tried to divert their son's attention from auto racing in his early teens, his parents realized after the 1995 championship season that there was no way to pull their son away from racing. Casey had a clearer vision as to what his future would hold, and it most definitely involved racing on four wheels. He has been quoted as saying, "I was well aware of the risks I was taking to pursue a career in racing. I saw my dad struggle through good years and bad years. Racing is one of those careers which requires commitment and 110 percent effort all of the time."

Casey continued to develop his skills and work through the ranks, and in 1996 he made his Indy Lights Championship Series debut at the Cleveland Grand Prix, finishing eighth. He competed full-time in the Indy Lights Championship Series in 1997, and within two years, he finished second in the championship points standings, losing by only 14 points. He scored 11 top-10 finishes, eight top-five finishes and four podium finishes, including second-place finishes at Milwaukee and Michigan. He was also the fourth driver in Indy Lights series history to complete every lap in a single season. Casey continued competing in the Indy Lights series through 2000 and won his first race at the Grand Prix of Houston that October.

Also in 2000, Mears began testing IndyCars for multiple teams, and in October, he was offered a chance to drive a third entry for Team Rahal in the CART Series at California Speedway. He qualified 15th, led 10 laps and finished fourth in his CART debut. Going into the 2001 season, Mears competed in three Indy Racing League events before switching to CART as replacement driver for the injured Alex Zanardi. Casey made four starts in the CART series, recording one top-10 finish.

October 2001 marked Casey's stock car debut in an ARCA series race at Talladega Superspeedway. Driving a Welliver-Jesel Motorsports car, Mears scored a ninth-place finish. Prior to the ARCA race, his only previous stock car experience was a few testing sessions he had done with Chip Ganassi Racing in 2000. By the end of the 2001 racing season, Mears made his first Busch Series start at Homestead-Miami Speedway and was named driver for the Welliver-Jesel Motorsports No. 66 for the 2002 Busch Series season.

The 2002 season was Casey's first full-time racing season in the Busch Series, and he successfully posted one top-five finish, two top-10 finishes and finished 21st in the overall standings. At the end of the season, Chip Ganassi Racing came knocking and lured Casey away from Welliver-Jessel to drive the No. 41 Target Dodge in the upcoming 2003 Winston Cup season. In his rookie year in Winston Cup racing, he failed to land a top-10 finish, ending the season close to the bottom of the standings in 35th place and ranked fifth out of seven drivers in the rookie standings.

Casey scored better in the Busch Series that same year, running 14 Busch Series races and recording one top-five finish, four top-10 results and one pole start. Mears also competed in four ARCA races during the 2003 season, winning three of them to give him his first wins in a stock car. The additional driving assignments helped

Mears adjust to stock car racing after competing in open-wheel racing in 2002.

Casey put in a strong performance throughout 2004, earning his first career Winston Cup top-five finish at Watkins Glen International. He was also able to follow in the tire-treads of his Uncle Rick, winning the pole position in track-record time at Indianapolis Motor Speedway on August 6, 2004. He won his first career pole just one week earlier at Pocono, making him the first driver since 1964 to post his first two career Nextel Cup poles in consecutive races.

While securing one top-five and nine top-10 finishes in the 2004 Cup Series, Mears also competed in 17 Busch Series races, including the race at California Speedway where he captured the race pole and went on to earn a career-best finish of second in the Busch Series. In his 17 starts in a Busch car, Mears accumulated one top-five and six top-10 finishes.

The 2005 Cup season was a roller-coaster ride for the kid from California. He watched two potential victories at Texas and Homestead (where he led 75 laps) disintegrate after late-race cautions. But he was able to finish the season on a high note, accumulating three top-five and nine top-10 finishes, including five top-10s in the final nine races.

Going into 2006, Casey celebrated his fourth season on the NASCAR Nextel Cup circuit, having steadily improved on his first three years with

Chip Ganassi Racing. All this effort prepared him for the pressure that goes along with driving the famed Texaco Star car. Many talented drivers have driven the No. 42 on the NASCAR circuit, including the legendary Davey Allison, Kenny Irwin, Ricky Rudd and Dale Jarrett, who still drives in Cup races in the No. 88. Having grown up around racing, Casey has many memories of Texaco/Havoline, especially the sponsor's relationship with Mario and Michael Andretti. Casey seems to be on a personal quest to restore the sponsor's heritage and long history of on-track success with the big red-and-black car.

Although Casey has a busy racing schedule as well as sponsor commitments and fan gatherings, he does allocate plenty of downtime to pursue the hobbies and pastimes that he feels are needed to live a well-balanced life. Apart from enjoying spending time with his family, especially at his favorite restaurant in Bakersfield (Luigi's Italian Ristoranti), he loves watching football and any form of racing. Casey also likes tinkering with his portable DVD player (yes, he's a bit of a tech-head) on which he frequently plays his favorite movie, The Last Samurai. As well, he spends time lounging around his pool or on his pontoon boat. In fact, he's happy to be anywhere there are palm trees and a beachfront. He also spends a lot of time polishing and caring for his most prized possession, his '61 Impala.

At one time, Casey dated the lovely Brittany Glover, daughter of Chip Ganassi's team manager Tony Glover, but things appeared to have fizzled out, and he is very much the single lad on the track these days. Instead, he tunes in to favorite musician, Jack Johnson, and continues to amass female fans and admirers who never fail to voice their adoration at trackside.

Chapter Eight

Brian Vickers

DATE OF BIRTH: October 24, 1983
BIRTHPLACE: Thomasville, North Carolina
RESIDES: Charlotte, North Carolina
DRIVES: No. 25 GMAC/ditech.com Chevrolet

Brian Vickers began his racing "career" at age eight, when he could be found weekends driving around his parents' yard on his dad's lawn-mower. He purchased his first go-kart with allowance money he earned cutting lawns, and he was racing go-karts by age 10. Brian eventually left go-kart racing as a three-time national champion after accumulating 83 career victories. Not bad for a 15-year-old.

Within five years, he graduated to the Allison Legacy Cars Series in 1998, and while driving in the Allison series, he celebrated five wins in just one season before advancing to NASCAR's Weekly Racing Series. The 16-year-old driver continued to impress. By the end of 1999, Brian Vickers had six late-model wins and 11 pole awards, one of the most impressive career starts of the modern era.

He was *Motorsports Magazine*'s 1999 Rising Star of the Year and won the Most Popular Driver award at Tri-County Speedway. In 2000, Vickers won the Rookie of the Year title while racing in USAR (United Speed Alliance Racing)—he was just 17 years old—adding another four wins during that year. In his first year in ProCup, Vickers won two races and became the youngest winner in series history, also taking home Rookie of the Year honors at the banquet. In 2001, Vickers once again captured two ProCup wins and finished second in the point standings.

Vickers debuted in the Busch Series in 2001 at Milwaukee, but an early accident took him out of contention after just 54 laps. Brian competed in three more Busch Series races in 2001, driving the EMP No. 40 Dodge, which he took to a career-best seventh place at Richmond International Raceway after starting way back in 38th position in the grid. He went on to make 21 Busch starts in 2002 with his family-owned team.

In the midst of all his racing activities, Brian was able to graduate with honors from Trinity High School in North Carolina in May 2002, the same year he won the 2002 USAR ProCup Rookie of the Year award. But his early dedication forced him to skip his high school prom to compete in a Busch Series race at Bristol Motor Speedway in Tennessee.

A little known fact about Brian is that teammate and former NASCAR champion Terry Labonte used to drive him to high school. One can only imagine the conversations the two racers enjoyed—as well as the thrill of having a champion racer as your chauffeur!

The 5'11" redhead from Thomasville, North Carolina, signed up with Hendrick Motorsports for the 2003 NASCAR Busch Series, competing in his first full season. Vickers not only won three races, but he also claimed the Busch Series championship for Hendrick Motorsports for the first time and became NASCAR's youngest-ever champion at age 20.

Going into the 2004 season, Brian Vickers had already been behind the wheel enough to be considered a veteran. With Team GMAC and crew chief Lance McGrew supporting him and giving him the machinery and tools needed to win, Brian was gaining popularity along with his unprecedented successes both on and off the track. On top of his racing, he began appearing on TV with post-race commentaries and state-of-the-sport opinion pieces.

Vickers competed in all 36 of the 2004 NASCAR Nextel Cup events driving his black No. 25 GMAC/ditech.com Chevrolet, ending the season with two pole positions, four top-10 finishes and a 25th-place result in the point standings.

Much of Brian's success in 2003 was due to the support of crew chief Lance McGrew, who helped Vickers secure the Busch Series championship. When Vickers moved over to the Nextel Cup Series, McGrew chose to stay with the Busch car for Hendrick Motorsports. But in 2005, McGrew finally moved over to Nextel and was reunited with his young driver and named crew chief of Brian's No. 25 team. Vickers has often being quoted as saying how much he depends on Lance: "There's a level of communication I have with him that I've never had before with a crew chief in my career. He's intelligent, and we have a good understanding of one another."

Throughout the 2004 and 2005 seasons, Brian made numerous appearances on SpeedTV's popular *Inside Nextel Cup* show with host Dave Despain and the show's regular co-hosts, fellow drivers Michael Waltrip and Ken Schrader. Brian offered his perspective on weekly race recaps and analysis. Apart from his easy-going delivery and sly sense of humor, Brian's movie-star good looks make him a natural in front of the camera. In 2004, Brian was featured in an episode of *NASCAR Drivers: 360* on the FX cable network, and even the edgy MTV music network came calling and invited him to guest on its popular *Total Request Live* in 2004.

For all the media exposure and trackside successes, Brian maintains a simple, down-to-earth lifestyle. When he can get away from the track, he plays golf, a popular (and safe) time-waster for many of the drivers, and he has become a skilled video gamer. During his downtime, he also reads extensively—he loved *The DaVinci Code* and the *Lord of the Rings* books—and listens to his favorite recording artists including Eminem, Nirvana, Limp Bizkit, Linkin Park, Nelly and P. Diddy. Away from the track, Brian drives his Chevy Tahoe and a cool Corvette.

Brian Vickers' name already appears in a number of record books, and as his career grows, many more of his records will likely be added. He was the sixth-youngest driver to compete in a Daytona 500 (20 years, 3 months, 22 days). He won the 2003 NASCAR Busch Series championship, becoming NASCAR's youngest-ever champion. He's listed as the youngest driver in USAR ProCup Series history to record a win (at the USA International Speedway on June 6, 2000, when he was just 17). He started five Cup Series events in 2003, qualifying in the top-five four times.

The 2005 season was another breakthrough year for Brian. He secured five top-five finishes and ten top-10 finishes in the Nextel Cup series, six top-10 qualifying starts in the Busch series and won the Lowe's Nextel Open race in May.

To help him stay in shape for the grueling demands of racing in both the Nextel and Busch series, a team nutritionist and trainers set out specific exercise programs to coach Brian through the season. Brian also likes to eat healthy, favoring Thai cuisine as well as sushi. He is single but admits to having a girlfriend. Brian loves meeting his fans and spends hours during race weekends signing autographs, posing for photos and meeting many of the younger fans who are thrilled to meet their hero. Brian recently got involved in an American youth fundraising program, where participants attend luncheons with community leaders and celebrities. He sees his involvement as an opportunity to have a positive impact on youngsters in danger of dropping out of school.

With an impressive 4.43 GPA, Brian was able to strike a great balance in his life, something he also encourages his fans to do. He loved racing enough that he had to do well in school—according to the rules set down by his parents, Brian wasn't allowed to race if he didn't get good grades. Brian Vickers makes an excellent role model for younger race fans, proving that you can "go for it" and be a winner in all aspects of your life—it just takes a bit of work and belief in yourself.

Chapter Nine

Ryan Newman

DATE OF BIRTH: December 8, 1977

BIRTHPLACE: South Bend, Indiana

RESIDES: Sherrills Ford, North Carolina

DRIVES: No. 12 Alltel/Mobil Oil Dodge Charger

Ryan Newman has the perfect background to excel in the technological world of 21st century stock car racing—he graduated from Purdue University in August 2001 with a degree in vehicle structure engineering—and it seems that he always has one of the fastest qualifying cars. Each year since 2002, Newman has scored 34 poles to lead the Cup series, earning him the nickname "Rocketman."

He and Penske crew chief Matt Borland are the first driver and crew chief team in NASCAR history to both have engineering degrees. In each of Newman's four seasons of Cup series racing, they have never finished lower than seventh in the final points standings.

As a 15-year-old, Newman began racing in 1993, winning the Michigan State Midget Championship and the AAMS Midget Series championship as well as Rookie of the Year. He was again awarded the USAC Midget Series Rookie of the Year honor in 1995 and followed that with the USAC Silver Crown Series Rookie of the Year award in 1996. In 1997, Newman was sixth in USAC Silver Crown points and won two midget feature races at Indy Raceway Park and the inaugural race at Pikes Peak International Raceway. Newman bettered his season standings in the USAC Silver Crown Series in 1998, scoring 11 top-10 finishes in 13 races and finishing the year third in points. He captured three consecutive midget series wins at the end of the season—all this before reaching the age of 21! Oh yes, and he was also inducted to the Quarter-Midget Hall of Fame.

Newman's association with Roger Penske, for whom now he drives the No. 12 Alltel Dodge, began in 2000 when he competed in the ARCA RE/MAX Series, posting three wins and two poles in five ARCA events for the motorsports icon. Ryan made his Cup debut at the end of the season in November at Phoenix. He also had 32 combined starts in the USAC Silver Bullet, midget and sprint car series, notching up two wins, 16 top-five results, 18 top-10 finishes and seven poles.

In 2001, Newman joined the Penske Racing South team, competing in two Automobile Racing Club of America (ARCA) races, 15 Busch Series races and seven Winston Cup races. His first career

Winston Cup pole came at the Lowe's Motor Speedway Coca-Cola 600, and he posted his first NASCAR victory in his ninth start at the Busch Series' NAPAonline.com 250 at Michigan International Speedway. That same season, he earned six Busch poles in only 14 starts. Over in the ARCA Series, he won the season opening Advance Auto Parts 200 at Daytona International Speedway and captured the pole in the inaugural event at Kansas.

The 2002 season marked the Rocketman's rookie year running a full-time Winston Cup series. During the season, he won six poles, breaking Davey Allison's 1987 rookie record of five. By the end of the year, Newman had racked up 16 top-five and 25 top-10 starts, 22 top-10 and 14 top-five finishes and a win at Loudon, New Hampshire, after starting from the pole. He finished the season sixth in the overall points standings and was named Rookie of the Year. He also became the only the second rookie ever to win the all-star race at Lowe's.

Newman started teaching the old dogs some new tricks in 2003, winning a series-high eight races and scoring 17 top-five and 22 top-10 finishes and nabbing 11 poles. Unfortunately, he also had seven DNFs and finished sixth in points for the second consecutive year. His outstanding achievements that season brought Ryan several other honors, including Speed Channel's Driver of the Year, the NMPA Richard Petty Driver of the Year award, the Benny Kahn/*Daytona Beach News Journal* Driver of the Year and the *Sporting News'* Dale Earnhardt Toughest Driver of the Year. It also brought him a huge payday of nearly $5 million from the Cup series alone.

The next year was special for Ryan—he married longtime love, Krissie Boyle. Not only that, but back on the track, he earned the annual Bud Pole Award a third straight year, becoming the first driver in nearly 20 years to achieve such a feat. Ryan also won two Cup races, one at Michigan International Speedway and the second one at Dover International Speedway, and earned a total of nine pole positions, the most of any driver. He led all competitors with 25 top-10 starts and finished out the season with 11 top-five and 14 top-10 finishes, placing seventh in the inaugural Nextel Cup point standings. Not a bad honeymoon!

Ryan scored his fourth consecutive Bud Pole Award in 2005 after posting a season total of eight poles. He also scored a Nextel Cup Series victory at New Hampshire International Speedway in September and finished the season with eight top-five and 16 top-10 finishes, this time placing sixth in the points standings for the team's second appearance in the Chase for the Cup.

But Ryan is not focused completely on his career. He takes time out of his race schedule to get in some serious fishing as well as to work on his growing collection of vintage autos, in particular his 1950s Chryslers.

Together, Ryan and Krissie run the Ryan Newman Foundation. The organization's main focus is caring for unwanted cats and dogs and helping to provide adequate care for them in shelters and pounds. Ryan helped fund the construction of the Catawba County Humane Society shelter (in North Carolina) near where he lives. During the aftermath of Hurricane Katrina in 2005, Krissie went down to the various disaster areas herself to bring relief and rescue to the thousands of stranded pets and livestock. The foundation also brought media attention to the desperate plight of animals left behind when their human companions fled for their lives or were killed.

Ryan and Krissie own three dogs: Digger, a German Shepherd–Doberman mix, Harley, a Labrador-Boxer cross, and Mopar, the biggest of the bunch, who is a Great Dane–Labrador mix. The Newmans also authored a fun book that hit the bookstore shelves in spring '06 called *Pit Row Pets*, featuring stories of Ryan's fellow drivers and their four-legged companions, with all of the profits benefiting free spaying and neutering clinics and no-kill shelters.

Like that other famous Newman couple (Paul Newman and Joanne Woodward), Ryan and Krissie share their good fortune with others, and that makes Ryan a champion in anyone's books.

Chapter Ten

Jeff Gordon

DATE OF BIRTH: August 4, 1971

BIRTHPLACE: Vallejo, California

RESIDES: Mooresville, North Carolina and
Boca Raton, Florida

DRIVES: No. 24 DuPont Chevrolet

No other driver has brought the razzle-dazzle to the sport like Jeff Gordon. Although he's slight in stature, he has arguably become the biggest presence on the circuit in the past 20 years. His good looks and charm, combined with his unbelievable success on the track, were instant magnets for the Hollywood set, and he has always been surrounded by the most beautiful female fans and admirers. Sponsors tripped over themselves in the rush to join his team, and Madison Avenue has heaped rewards upon him in excess of $15 million per year. In fact, he has become an industry unto himself, with a recently launched racing school, co-ownership in other Cup cars and a vineyard that has just produced its first crop of Chardonnay, as well as various charitable foundations and educational programs. He's also become a champion poker player, and if you look really closely, you'll see a royal flush fanned out across the back of his race helmet.

But the normally humble golden boy has survived many dark moments too, the hardest of which must have been the loss of his Hendrick Motorsports teammates in a terrible October 2004 plane crash just outside of Martinsville, Virginia. The tragedy took 10 friends who made up an important part of the race team. In 2005, when Gordon took the checkered flag at Martinsville just one year later, the Hendrick team, the entire pit area and people in the grandstands and trackside reversed their ballcaps in tribute to the late Ricky Hendrick, who used to wear his headgear the same way. Gordon was moved to tears.

Jeff married a former Miss Winston Cup in the mid-'90s, but after seven years of a seemingly happy marriage, his wife Brooke filed for divorce in 2002. The legal process became so nasty that Jeff became tabloid fodder for months. Although Brooke demanded half of his reported $48.8 million in assets, the suit eventually ended in June 2003 with Brooke settling for a reported $15.5 million.

Gordon eventually recovered from the emotional stress that took its toll on his driving, thanks to a newfound faith and several brief relationships, including one with model Amanda Church. For the past two years, he has been seriously involved with a beautiful brunette, Belgian model-actress Ingrid Vandebosch. He reportedly met his latest interest while on the set of the movie *Taxi*, in which Ingrid portrayed a bank robber and Jeff made an uncredited cameo appearance. From early in the 2005 season, Ingrid was often seen trackside on race day cheering for Jeff.

Jeff's interest in racing started when he was barely a year old. He, his older sister, Kim, and his recently divorced mother, Carol, attended a race at Vallejo Speedway with stock car fan John Bickford. By the time Jeff turned four, his mother married Bickford, who took the toddler under his "racing wing" and bought him a BMX bicycle followed by a quarter-midget race car when he turned five.

The youngster raced the dirt tracks in his home area as well as traveling farther afield to Rio Linda on weekends. The first time he climbed into a real race car was at Rio Linda, and his stepdad sensed immediately that Jeff would become a race driver. Gordon drove practice laps in his quarter-midget as soon as it rolled off the delivery truck. Every night, Bickford took the car out after he returned home from work, and Jeff drove it lap after lap. He couldn't seem to get enough, and by age eight, he'd won his first quarter-midget championship. Two more championships followed, and by the early 1980s, he had won four class championships in go-karts.

Jeff Gordon was born to race. Before he could even read or write he was taking the checkered flag, racing his quarter-midget every weekend wherever a race was held. Sometimes the family put on over 1000 miles on round trips to and from the races, but both Bickford and mom Carol could clearly see their son's potential as a stock car star.

Jeff was winning just about every race he entered, and by age nine, he was defeating drivers aged 17 and older and was constantly improving and reaching higher levels of skill and daring. Bickford claims that racing was Jeff's idea, even at such a young age, but both he and Carol made sure he was safe at all times.

Young Gordon's California racing career peak was the Quarter Midget National Championships. At just 11 years old, he was winning steadily, but the Quarter Midget Championship was a special series. Gordon was confident but cautious, and he knew there was always a chance his lucky streak would end and he could lose—but he didn't.

With this success, it was apparent to everyone that Jeff's future was sealed: he would be a racer. But the family had a major decision to make. By 1985, with Jeff's career plans laid out, his parents knew he could not get the competition he needed to develop or become known as long as they stayed in California. He needed to race against more mature drivers, but because of age restrictions in the state, he couldn't do that without moving. The family had reached a crossroads where they had to make a commitment to Jeff and help advance his career. So they uprooted and moved to Florida. Then, in 1986, they relocated to Pittsboro, Indiana, near Indianapolis.

Open-wheel racing was popular in the Midwest, and there were plenty of tracks in the Indianapolis area. And with his parents' permission, Jeff could legally race sprint cars in Indiana. Living in rural Pittsboro, the family was near the car chassis builders and several racetracks, but things were far from easy. Many fans and most of the media have long been under the impression that Gordon was a rich kid from California born with a silver spoon in his mouth, but that was just not the case. Going from race to race with Jeff, the family slept in pickup trucks, and Bickford, an auto-parts worker, worked with Jeff to make their own car parts.

At 16 years old, Jeff joined the United States Auto Club (USAC), becoming the youngest person to ever get a license with the group. He triumphed in three sprint car track championships before he was old enough to earn his regular state-issued driver's license.

But he still couldn't find the competition that would challenge him and improve his skills, so in the late '80s, Bickford took him down to Australia and New Zealand to compete in sprint car races. All the hard work and mileage paid off when he was declared the 1989 USAC Midget Rookie of the Year.

Even though his passion was racing, which he lived and breathed, Jeff still had to go to school like other "normal" kids. He attended Tri-West High School in nearby Lizton, Indiana, where he was voted prom king, and he graduated in 1989. Graduation day for Jeff was doubly demanding and exciting; he received his diploma then quickly changed into his racing gear for a dirt-track race that same night. He often had to leave school early or even cut classes on Fridays so he could head off to be in time to race, and by graduation, he'd already won more than 100 races.

He won the 1990 USAC Midget Championship, and that same year, Gordon ran 21 USAC midget car races. He was the fastest qualifier 10 times, won nine races, and at age 19, became the youngest midget class champion ever.

He then advanced to USAC's Silver Crown Division, which runs cars that are similar to midgets and sprints but a lot bigger. At just 20 years old, he became the youngest driver to win the Silver Crown championship. Bickford suggested that Jeff go to Rockingham, North Carolina, and attend the famed Buck Baker's driving school, which groomed drivers for the big race—NASCAR stock cars. The young driver was already a media darling. TV sports network ESPN produced a story about Jeff's experiences there, and in return for the publicity, Baker taught Gordon free of charge. After he took his first lap in a stock car, Jeff realized that he had found the cars he wanted to race, and there was no looking back.

The 1991 season was Gordon's breakthrough year. After he won the USAC Silver Crown title, he quickly moved up into the Busch Grand National competition driving the No. 1 Carolina Ford owned by Bill Davis. He took Rookie of the Year honors. The car was sponsored by the Baby Ruth candy bar company. In 1992, Jeff captured a record 11 pole positions.

The same year, Winston Cup car owner Rick Hendrick noticed Gordon driving an extremely loose race car around Atlanta Motor Speedway, and he nervously waited and watched for the driver to lose control and wreck. But Jeff went on to win the race, and Hendrick instructed his general manager to sign the budding young star to a Winston Cup contract immediately.

In a move that still reverberates badly with racing media and splits the fans' respect, Gordon signed with Hendrick Motorsports in 1992 to drive for car owner Rick Hendrick. Gordon's mentor and first car owner Bill Davis had expected Jeff to drive for him when his team moved up to Winston Cup. But rather than move into Winston Cup competition with Davis' somewhat average team that might not be strong enough to qualify every weekend, Jeff decided to sign with Hendrick, who offered him the deal of a lifetime and put him into the elite circle of NASCAR teams. To this day, many feel that Gordon's abandonment of Davis, the man who believed in him and basically handed him his career on a silver platter, was the ultimate insult, and barely a post-race commentary goes by without someone mentioning that moment in Gordon's career. It's a permanent black mark on an otherwise incredible record.

Gordon's Winston Cup career started out strong in 1993, with the rookie first winning the Gatorade 125-mile qualifying race for the Daytona 500 and then winning the heart of Miss Winston, Brooke Sealy, in Victory Lane. The pair eventually married in 1994.

Over the following years, he chalked up win after win and garnered worldwide attention when he won the inaugural Brickyard 400 at Indianapolis in August 1994. He finished eighth in the standings, and although he showed continued improvement, no one was prepared for his outstanding 1995 season: seven victories culminating with his first Winston Cup title. Gordon was the toast of New York City in December 1995 at the NASCAR Awards Banquet. He was no longer the wunderkind. He'd proved himself a true champion.

In the middle of his championship year, though, Gordon asked his mother and stepfather to step down as his managers. He hired Bob Brannan in May 1995 as manager of his business affairs, a move that distanced his parents and reminded many of his earlier split from Bill Davis.

The next few years brought untold wealth and triumph on the track along with more television appearances such as guesting on *Saturday Night Live*, *Live With Regis and Kathy Lee (*and later, *Regis and Kelly)* and *Late Night with David Letterman.* (Letterman is not only a racing fan but also a co-owner of a race team.)

Pepsi came on board as associate sponsor in 1997. In an ironic twist, Gordon won the Coca-Cola 600 on Memorial Day weekend. Later, he became only the second driver in history to win the Winston Million when he won the Southern 500 at Darlington Raceway. In addition, he became the only driver to win the Southern 500 three years in a row. The rest of the '97 season was inconsistent, but Jeff was still able to win the Winston Cup title by a mere 14 points over Dale Jarrett.

Gordon has won four Cup championships in total and is likely to take a few more before he hangs up his helmet. In the past few seasons, he's been criticized for spending more time in front of the cameras than behind the wheel, and his recent lack of wins and consistency has been attributed to his "A-list" lifestyle that has alienated him from many of the traditional, down-home fans. But with a new crew chief, young Steve Letarte, leading him back to Victory Lane towards the end of the 2005 season and into the 2006 Cup chase, the No. 24 will no doubt once again be in the hunt for clean air, out front of the pack once again.

Chapter Eleven

Tony Stewart

DATE OF BIRTH: May 20, 1971

BIRTHPLACE: Columbus, Indiana

RESIDES: Columbus and Rushville, Indiana

DRIVES: No. 20 Home Depot Chevrolet

Whoever said "you can't go home again" hadn't met Tony "Smoke" Stewart, two-time Nextel Cup Champion and poster boy for anger management.

Since his 2000 Watkin's Glen run-in with rival Jeff Gordon, followed by an obscenity-laden tirade during the post-race press conference, Stewart had become the bully of NASCAR, always playing the blame-game after any race mishap. His temper has gotten the best of him on many occasions. Some call it passion or single-mindedness, but Stewart's fiery bluntness has often led to collisions with the media, fans and fellow drivers.

But he recently underwent anger management therapy with the help of a psychologist and decided to move out of the spotlight of stock car racing's capital, Charlotte, North Carolina, and go back home to Columbus, Indiana. He even purchased his childhood home, located only two blocks from his old high school. Now, safe in the company of old friends, family and a newly acquired dog, he has said how comfortable and calming it feels to get back to his roots, and he is a lot happier.

The opening races of the 2006 season have certainly shown a mellower Smoke after the previous season's almost weekly eruptions against one or the other of his competitors. During one post-race interview in 2005, he managed to insult three drivers in one sentence, including calling No. 16's Greg Biffle "an idiot." Biffle refused to rise to the bait and simply shrugged off the slur as just another example of Stewart's behavioral problems.

But Stewart has always been in a league of his own, right from the start. Tony started racing go-karts at age seven, with his father, Nelson, acting as his crew chief. Dad never let his boy settle for second best, and to this day, he cheers on his son at the races whenever he can, still encouraging Tony to be better, faster and the most skillful driver he can be.

In 1980, at age eight, Stewart won his first championship, a four-cycle rookie junior championship at the Columbus Fairgrounds. Two national karting championships followed: the 1983 International Karting Federation Grand National championship and the 1987 World Karting Association National championship. By 1989, Stewart transitioned from go-karts to open-wheel vehicles, racing three-quarter midgets before graduating to the USAC ranks in 1991 and winning Rookie of the Year honors.

The 1994 season brought his first USAC championship; he won five times in 22 starts in the national midget category. Then, in 1995, Stewart made USAC history by winning the Triple Crown: he won the national midget, sprint and Silver Crown titles all in the same year, something never before accomplished by any driver. That success earned Stewart a ride in the fledgling IndyCar series, and after earning Rookie of the Year honors in 1996, Stewart topped that by winning the series championship the following year. In 1997, he again won the IndyCar championship, which led to his securing 22 rides in the 1998 Busch Series races with Joe Gibbs Racing.

The Nextel Cup Series was all that was left for Stewart to conquer, and in 1999, Tony blasted the field wide open. He had a remarkable season, winning three races as well as competing in both the Indianapolis 500 and the Coca-Cola 600 on the same day. Stewart started his double duty in a Home Depot–sponsored Indy car at Indianapolis. He then flew to Concord, North Carolina, to compete in the Coca-Cola 600 that evening in his No. 20 Home Depot Chevy, becoming the first driver to complete both races in the same day and finishing ninth and fourth respectively. All in all, he chalked up 1090 miles in one day. He also showed great courage in one of the Gatorade Twin 125 races when he became involved in a duel with Dale Earnhardt Sr. for the win. The Intimidator eventually won, but Tony impressed many fans and racing aficionados with his performance. He finished that first year an unprecedented fourth in the standings, the highest points finish by a rookie since 1972 and only bested by James Hylton, who finished second as a first-timer in 1966. It's no wonder Stewart won the Rookie of the Year title.

He repeated his famous double-duty feat in 2001, driving a Target/Home Depot Indy car for Chip Ganassi at the Indy 500 and finishing sixth before jetting off again to Concord, where he placed third in the Coca-Cola 600. His newly acquired Tony Stewart Motorsports team won the 2001 World of Outlaws championship in their rookie year and has since finished second in points three times. Stewart also owns numerous USAC teams that compete in the sprint, midget and Silver Crown divisions, winning championships and four USAC owner's titles.

The 2001 season got off to a scary start when Tony was involved in a nasty crash in the Daytona 500. His car spun and flipped over several times, but he managed to walk away unscathed and went on to win three more races, running near the front for the majority of the season. Although statistics prove he had actually run a worse season than 2000, he still made runner-up to Jeff Gordon for the Cup championship.

As usual for Tony, though, the season was not without controversy. Gordon pulled a "bump and run" on the No. 20 to gain a better finish at Bristol, which led to Stewart getting some post-race vengeance by spinning Gordon out on pit road. Stewart was fined and placed on probation by NASCAR but then got into even more trouble at Daytona when he confronted a race official after ignoring a black flag. At the same race, he also got into an incident with a reporter when he kicked a tape recorder. The volatile driver was given another fine and an even longer probation period.

As luck would have it, the same official confronted Tony again at the race in Talladega after he refused to wear a mandated HANS device (head-and-neck restraint). Stewart was not allowed to practice until he agreed to wear one and only managed to get out on the track after his crew chief intervened and convinced him to wear the restraint.

In 2002, things started out even worse than the previous season, with his Daytona 500 lasting only two laps because of a blown engine. He managed to win twice early in the year, but he stood only seventh in points at the halfway mark of the season. The second half of his Cup run was plagued by another altercation with a photographer after the Brickyard 400. Smoke was back on probation for the rest of the season, but he rallied and went on to win the next race immediately after being disciplined, and in the final races, he finished consistently in the top five. At the end of the year, Stewart held off veteran Mark Martin to win his first Winston Cup championship.

As defending champion, Tony managed to drop the brutish on- and off-track attitude and had a relatively incident-free 2003 season. He drove a Chevrolet instead of his usual Pontiac, but he had his worst Cup season ever, although it was still good enough for seventh in the points. He only won twice that year but led more laps than he had the previous season, and he was highly competitive in the final races of the year.

Late the following year, Stewart became the owner of one of the most legendary short tracks in America, Eldora Speedway, located in Rossburg, Ohio—a half-mile dirt track where Tony began racing in 1991. He continues to race there in special events alongside other Nextel Cup drivers and dirt track legends. He also makes the occasional cameo on other dirt tracks, appearing regularly at an ARCA race on dirt and at many midget car events, USAC's Turkey Night Grand Prix and the indoor Chili Bowl Midget Nationals.

Also in 2004, Stewart teamed with British racing businessman Andy Wallace and NASCAR track mate Dale Earnhardt Jr. in a Boss Motorsports Chevrolet to take fourth place in the 24 Hours of Daytona sports car race. The final result does not really show their true performance, however. They dominated the race until the last two hours, when the Chevy's suspension cracked. Then, with just 15 minutes left in the race, Stewart was behind the wheel when one of the rear wheels came off, finally ending their run to the checkered flag and leaving them in fourth place.

Overachiever Stewart added a second Nextel Cup to his trophy collection in 2005, joining an elite club of just 14 drivers in the past 50 years who have won multiple Cup Series titles. Stewart earned five wins, scored three poles and scored a career-best 17 top-five finishes and 25 top-10 showings, but it was his emotional Brickyard 400 win at Indianapolis Motor Speedway that seemed to affect him the most. The Columbus, Indiana native grew up hoping to race at Indianapolis, and the win marked the fulfillment of a dream that had eluded him for years. When the 2005 season ended, he was also a lot richer financially with a record payday of $13,578,168, including $6,173,633 for winning the championship, giving him the largest season earnings total in NASCAR history.

And he needed the money because the fines kept coming. On August 16, Tony was fined $5000 and placed on probation until December 31 for running into Brian Vickers' car after the completion of the Busch Series Zippo 200 at Watkins Glen International. Possibly in an attempt to work off excess energy and diffuse any leftover anger, Stewart began a tradition of climbing the safety fence separating the fans from the track after each victory. But after one huff-and-puff ascent, he was quoted as saying, "I'm too fat for this," and promptly purchased nearly $20,000 worth of exercise equipment to remedy the problem.

Tony does, however, have a softer side that he reserves for his philanthropic works. He has formed his own charitable organization—the Tony Stewart Foundation. Run by his mother, Pam Boas, the charity was formed in 2003 to raise funds for organizations that help care for critically ill children and to lend support to families of race car drivers who have been injured while racing.

He's also an animal lover. He has owned dogs, fish, a rabbit, an iguana and a cat, although he found he was allergic to cats and was forced to give up his small furry friend. But allergies aside, he even ended up with a really big feline—a tiger. A friend took him to Metrolina Wildlife Park in Rockwell, North Carolina, where he met the owner, Steve Macaluso, who took him along to meet the park's star residents, a family of tigers. The female had just delivered cubs, and when he was allowed to hold one of them, love blossomed. He was allowed to take the young cub home a short time later, and he named her Tangie. But she grew too much to handle, and he realized she needed to return to the park, where he visits her often.

Although he hopes to someday marry and raise a family, he has an on-again, off-again relationship with girlfriend Krista Dwyer. They share "custody" of Tony's pet Patas monkey, Mojo, who has apparently grown too big and rambunctious for the motorhome and now spends most of his time with Krista. Tony and Krista were engaged in May 1999, but a wedding date was never set, and the pair split a couple of years later. They have remained friends and even tried dating again seriously in 2004. But apart from the monkey, they don't appear to be sharing too much else in 2006.

Chapter Twelve

David Stremme

DATE OF BIRTH: June 19, 1977
BIRTHPLACE: South Bend, Indiana
DRIVES: No. 40 Coors Light/Lonestar Dodge

Stock car racing is a family affair for the Stremme clan. David's father, Lou, was a racer, as was his mother, Cindy. Young David worked on his parents' race cars, tinkering under the hood long before he could even drive himself. But he was never pushed into racing by his parents— it was just something that came naturally to him. David started competing locally against both of his parents, racing against his mother more often that his dad. The first year he drove competitively, she beat him to the checkered flag at nearly every event, but by the second year, David was leaving her in the dust.

The Stremmes always emphasized the importance of an education and insisted that good report cards equaled time behind the wheel. David did not disappoint them, and he has since developed into an astute young businessman and car owner himself.

David officially began his racing career in 1993 at age 15. He started driving street stocks and quickly scored his first victory at New Paris Speedway behind the wheel of his mother's race car. The young driver quickly moved on to late models, open-wheel modifieds and then to the NASCAR Southwest Series. He notched up win after win, earning Rookie of the Year titles and two track championships.

Things really started to click for Stremme in 2000, when he moved to the ASA Series. That first year, he competed in eight races, earning one pole and four top-10 finishes, but his big breakthrough came in 2002, his most successful season, when he scored four second-place finishes and won his first ASA race at Salem Speedway. His second ASA win came shortly afterwards at Indianapolis Raceway Park. David finished the season fourth in the points standings and earned the prestigious Pat Schaurer Memorial Rookie of the Year Award.

All these accomplishments drew the attention of the Chip Ganassi Racing organization and their driver talent coordinator, Lorin Ranier. Stremme was invited to Lakeland International Speedway to test alongside potential future CGRFS teammates Jamie McMurray and Casey Mears, and after an impressive display, he became the first racer signed to the team's driver development program.

Chip Ganassi convinced James Finch, the owner of the No. 1 Dodge in the Busch Series, to assign the car to David so he could drive some races for the team and get valuable seat time. It was a perfect match and an instant success. The rookie started 15th in his debut race at Nashville Superspeedway in April 2003, but he worked his way carefully through the field and finished a solid seventh. He then finished 14th in both of his next two starts before coming in sixth at Nazareth Speedway, where he led for 32 laps.

David continued to improve his position through-out the season, finishing fourth after starting third at Nashville in June, then duplicating that run at the Milwaukee Mile. He scored a 10th-place finish at Kentucky and a ninth at Memphis. Perhaps most amazing for a rookie, Stremme only had one DNF (did not finish), at Dover, and apart from that race, his worst-place finish was in 21st.

But car owner Finch wanted to put Jamie McMurray back into the car for the final two races, even though Stremme's performance had been consistent and he was in the middle of a hunt for the Busch Series Rookie of the Year. David was eventually forced out of the No. 1 Dodge and moved over to Braun Racing for the season's last two races. As a tongue-in-cheek payback to Finch, David's No. 30 unsponsored car was adorned with the decals "I Just Want to Race the Car." At Rockingham, he led 48 laps and finished fifth, and then for the final race at Miami, David drove the No. 30 Sport Clips Dodge home in 14th place—just enough to secure him the Rookie of the Year award. He drove in only 18 of the 34 races, becoming the first driver to win the title without competing full time in the series, a considerable feat that caught the attention of the media and fans.

The 2004 season dawned full of promise, and David was excited that his No. 32 TrimSpa Dodge team showed early signs of being a winner. Starting fourth on the grid and finishing sixth in the season opener at Daytona International Speedway, David was thrilled with the team effort. He scored his best qualifying effort to date at Rockingham, starting on the outside pole. He followed that with a third place at Las Vegas and a fifth at Darlington. But somehow, the team seemed to burn out, and despite winning his first career pole at Milwaukee and a second-place finish, the No. 32 gang found themselves finishing mid-pack, with a handful of top-10 places towards the end of the season.

Realizing something was wrong in the mix, Ganassi stepped in. He understood that owner Todd Braun wanted to put Shane Hmiel in the car. Forming an alliance with FitzBradshaw Racing, Ganassi put David into the No. 14 Navy Chevy instead. After a few solid finishes in the No. 14, by the end of 2004, David's 12th place at the season closer in Miami secured him a top-10 points ranking.

David worked hard in the Busch Series throughout the 2005 season, but luck was not on his side. He had nine DNFs during the season, many of which were because of right-front tire problems. But he still managed to complete some great runs, finishing third at Las Vegas and Talladega and fifth at Milwaukee and Indianapolis. The team's inconsistent performance hurt, and ultimately, those DNFs and fewer top-10 finishes left David out of championship contention with a 13th place in the points standings.

One bright light in that year came in June, when Ganassi announced that David would move over to the Cup series in 2006, driving the No. 40 Coors Light Dodge. David was given a ride in the No. 39 Navy Dodge at Chicagoland Speedway just to whet his appetite. He started 31st and finished 16th among a field of Cup veterans. In his four 2005 Cup starts, that was David's highest finish, but it didn't dampen his spirits—he was going to "the big show" next year, and after 13 years of racing, he was finally getting to fulfill his lifelong dream of racing in NASCAR's premier series.

But success has never gone to David's head. When his family's business expanded in 2004, he became the car owner for his brother Bobby in the ASA Late Model Series, and mom Cindy now manages. To thank his parents for all their support and guidance, he bought his father a new engine for his car as well as other maintenance equipment for the Stremme family garage.

David has kept his personal life private, but he has been rumored to have a steady girlfriend, Whitney. Track sources have remained tight-lipped, and little is known about the young lady who apparently lights up his life.

Chapter Thirteen

Kyle Busch

DATE OF BIRTH: May 2, 1985
BIRTHPLACE: Las Vegas, Nevada
RESIDES: Mooresville, North Carolina
DRIVES: No. 5 Kellogg's Chevrolet

Although he's the second-born son of Tom and Gaye Busch, Kyle has carved out a career made up of firsts in stock car racing. Starting at age 12, Kyle only took eight short years to reach the top of NASCAR's premier series, the Nextel Cup, emerging as the youngest race winner in history.

As an active six-year-old, Kyle had his first driving lessons go-karting around the cul-de-sac in Las Vegas where the Busch family lived. His dad had to work the throttle since Kyle was too short to reach the pedal, but once he grew tall enough to hit the gas on his own, Kyle's destiny was cast as a stock car driver—and a champion one at that.

All through his childhood years, Kyle apprenticed with his father and older brother Kurt in the family garage, learning how to build and repair race cars. By age 10, Kyle was a full-fledged mechanic and served as crew chief on his older brother's dwarf car team. In 1998, not longer after he celebrated his 13th birthday, Kyle started his own official driving career.

Because of his young age, his parents insisted that schoolwork had to be his first priority, and he didn't disappoint his family. He even became an honors student. But his heart lay with his extracurricular activity—auto racing. His parents taught him that if he wanted to race, he had to work on, repair and pay for his own cars, and he quickly learned that carelessness on the track proved expensive. A wrecked race car took a great deal of money and many hours to repair, and the car might not be ready in time for the next event. Kyle took great pride in his equipment and became known for his respect for his fellow drivers and their cars.

Between 1999 and 2001, Kyle scored more than 65 wins in the Legends series, logging two track championships at the "Bullring" at Las Vegas Motor Speedway before moving up to late models. Busch was on a winning streak that seemed as though it would never end. Whatever he drove, he won. He captured 10 victories in late-model competition at the Bullring in 2001, and his reputation spread to those in the know. Many of the big-name car owners in NASCAR were learning that Kurt Busch's kid brother was no little shrub.

In August 2001, at age 16, Kyle Busch made his Craftsman Truck Series debut at Indianapolis Raceway Park, driving as a replacement for Roush Racing after the team's two drivers were released midway in the season. He was the fastest in practice for the race at California Speedway in Fontana, California, but he was unceremoniously ejected from the track by CART officials because the American Racing Wheels 200 race was part of a racing weekend featuring the Marlboro 500 CART event. Kyle was dismissed from the garage because of an interpretation of the Master Settlement Agreement of 1998 that prohibited persons under 18 years of age from participating in events sponsored by tobacco companies. Six weeks after the incident, NASCAR also imposed a minimum age of 18 (starting in 2002) to prevent future incidents because Winston was the premier series sponsor.

When the age requirements were put in place, Kyle refused to be sidelined and switched to the American Speed Association (ASA) series, which had no such restrictions. The Midwest-based organization was instrumental in furthering Kyle's career with several well-publicized successes. Kyle finished eighth in the championship points for the 2002 ASA series, posting five top-five and 10 top-10 finishes in 20 starts. Kyle also graduated with honors a year early from Durango High School in Las Vegas.

On February 4, 2003, Kyle signed a contract to drive with Hendrick Motorsports and almost immediately found success on the track, winning his first Automobile Racing Club of America (ARCA) event at Nashville Superspeedway from the pole position. He followed that with a second victory at Kentucky Speedway in the next outing. That same year, he entered several Busch Series races behind the wheel of the No. 87 Ditech.com car for Hendrick Motorsports, scoring second place at Lowe's Motor Speedway in his first start. He finished the year with two more second-place finishes, three top-10 results and five top-10 qualifying efforts.

Kyle's first full-time season began in 2004. First, he took an ARCA victory in his first-ever start on the high banks of Daytona International Speedway on February 7. He also drove the Lowe's Busch Series car vacated by Brian Vickers, who had moved up to the Nextel Cup series. Kyle easily clinched Rookie of the Year honors in the series, dominating the field from the outset and becoming the youngest rookie ever at 19. His first top-10 finish of the season came at the second race in Rockingham, his first pole of the season in his fifth race, and he claimed his first victory at the Richmond International Raceway in May. In total, he scored five wins in 2004, finishing second in overall points to Martin Truex Jr.

In order to gain experience and seat time in NASCAR's premier series, Kyle managed to qualify for six Nextel Cup Series races. Late in the 2004 season, Kyle was selected by team owner Rick Hendrick to replace two-time Cup Series champion Terry Labonte in the famed No. 5 Kellogg's Chevrolet for 2005 and beyond.

The 19-year-old Kyle started the 2005 season with a record-setting pole at California Speedway in just his eighth career Nextel Cup Series start. He was exactly 19 years, 317 days old, which broke the record previously held by Donald Thomas, who was 20 years, 129 days old when he won the pole at Lakewood Speedway in Georgia on November 16, 1952. Thomas won that race and had remained the youngest winner in Cup Series history until Kyle won at California Speedway in September 2005. Kyle polished off his Nextel rookie year with another victory at Phoenix International Raceway in November, completing a season made up of one pole, nine top-five and 13 top-10 results, two wins and a 20th-place finish in the standings. He also won the Raybestos Rookie of the Year award for the second consecutive season and became the youngest winner of the award in the history of the Nextel Cup. Kyle Busch and Jeff Gordon are the only two Hendrick Motorsports drivers to win Rookie of the Year honors.

Kyle's full roster of records includes seven Raybestos Rookie records on the circuit, and he remains the youngest Rookie of the Year in the history of the program at 19. He tied the 2001 Busch Series Rookie of the Year record held by Greg Biffle for most wins (5) and most top-five results (16). Kyle Busch finished second in the 2004 Busch Series, the best championship finish ever by a rookie. In 2004, Kyle led 42 times in 21 races for a total of 1390.89 miles (1108 laps), the most by any driver in the Busch Series. For the first time since the program was created in 1989, a rookie led the most miles—Kyle led the most laps in seven races. And in 2005, he became the youngest Craftsman Truck Series winner in history at age 20 with his win at Lowe's Motor Speedway on May 20, 2005 (the record was previously held by the late Ricky Hendrick). Kyle accumulated three wins, seven top-five and nine top-10 finishes and a pole position in just 11 Craftsman Truck starts.

The 2006 season started off with a big bang for Kyle, who won the Sharpie Mini 300 at Bristol and four top-10 places in the season's first seven events. However, a dark cloud appeared on the younger Busch's horizon. On April 14, 2006, Kyle was ticketed for reckless driving in a suburb of Richmond, Virginia. The citation came five months after brother Kurt was ticketed for reckless driving in Arizona in November 2005, resulting in his suspension by Roush Racing for the final two races of the year and a mass of negative publicity from which he has yet to recover. Because of Kyle's misdemeanor charge, he had a mandatory court appearance scheduled for May 23, 2006, with the possibility of a year in jail.

He should, however, have not only his family standing by him when he pleads his case, but also his girlfriend, Erica Dewey, who Kyle has been dating for over a year. Erica is a real morale booster, having been active in the "Adopt A Soldier" program that matches soldiers stationed overseas with stateside pen pals. Hopefully, the beauty pageant winner won't be writing to her beau stationed behind bars.

Chapter Fourteen

Robby Gordon

DATE OF BIRTH: January 2, 1967

BIRTHPLACE: Bellflower, California

RESIDES: Cornelius, North Carolina and Anaheim Hills, California

DRIVES: No. 7 Jim Beam Chevrolet

Nicknamed "Flash" as a kid, Robby Gordon was racing motorbikes by age eight. Robby started his racing career in 1985 at age 16 when he won the first off-road race he entered at the Mickey Thompson Stadium in California. His first car was a red 1977 Chevy Blazer (two-wheel drive) that his father helped him customize. Robbie started out working in his father's feed yard raking chaff. After realizing that his son showed great potential for success on the track, Robby's father encouraged the youngster to expand his racing desires by teaming up with him the next year. With his dad's help, Robby won the SCORE/HDRA championship by taking the checkered flag at four off-road events.

After dominating the SCORE/HDRA Heavy Metal Off-Road series for four years, Robby decided to take his place in the IMSA series. Much to his dad's delight, he scored second place in points for the IMSA GTO standings that year. Throughout the season, he won numerous events as well as taking the pole position in his first stock car race at the ARCA event held at the Atlanta Motorspeedway, bringing him to the attention of several Winston Cup car owners.

Robby began racing professionally in 1990 and made his 1991 Winston Cup debut in the Daytona 500, racing for Jack Roush. He finished 18th. Throughout the early '90s, he raced in numerous leagues, including the Sports Car Club of America (SCCA) and the PPG Indy Car World Series, driving for the famed A.J. Foyt Racing team. He drove in his first Indianapolis 500 in 1993 and logged his first CART PPG Indy Car World Series victories at Phoenix and Detroit for Walker Racing in 1995.

Late in 1996, Robby routinely began to appear in NASCAR Winston Cup events, driving for the SABCO and DEI racing teams. In March 1997, he won his first NASCAR pole position in a cold-weather time trial at the Atlanta Motor Speedway. Later that same season, he impressed everyone with his driving expertise on the upstate New York Watkins Glen road course, finishing fourth, after which he flew off to the Brickyard and finished 12th at the famed Indianapolis 500.

Although he showed promise in the NASCAR series, for a while Robby lost interest in the big show and returned to a variety of other racing series where he was able to really push himself and hone his skills as a driver. That period of his racing career culminated in 1999, when he lost the lead of the Indianapolis 500 on the final lap. His car ran out of fuel, and Robby limped across the finish line to claim an anticlimactic fourth-place position.

Gordon returned to the Winston Cup series in 2000, competing in nearly 20 events, once again placing fourth at Watkins Glen and then taking a top-10 finish at Sears Point. With memories of the previous year's disaster at the Indy 500 still fresh, Robby returned to the Brickyard and scored a respectable sixth place—this time with a little bit of gas still in the fuel cell.

By 2002, a more mature Robby Gordon emerged as a full-time Winston Cup driver. He was named as the driver for RCR's No. 31 Cingular Chevrolet after the team's current driver was forced to undergo surgery. During the 2002 season, Robby finished third at Watkins Glen and completed what has become his customary "double hitter" by racing in both the Indianapolis 500 and Coca-Cola 600 in May. He managed to finish eighth at the Indy and 16th in Charlotte. Overall, not a bad season for Robby, who finished 20th in the Winston Cup points standings.

Going into 2003, Robby began to showcase his real abilities, especially on the road courses. He won at Watkins Glen and then dueled with Jeff Gordon to take a stunning victory at Sonoma, becoming the fourth driver to win both Winston Cup road races in a single year. He also proved himself a true stock car champion by placing first at New Hampshire. Robby finished out 2003 with an improved 16th place in points, but that was not truly reflective of the solid season that he and his team put together.

Robby enjoyed an infamous 2005 season, not so much for his driving but for his road rage on track. His most famous outburst came at New Hampshire in September shortly after an on-track incident involving Michael Waltrip. While the cars were under the caution flag so that track officials could clean up debris from Gordon's wrecked car, Robby walked out into the oncoming traffic and threw his helmet at Waltrip's driver-side window. Fortunately, he missed the open space and bounced the helmet off the roof. Even though NASCAR fined Gordon $35,000 and docked him 50 driver points, series officials had to love the publicity—as did the fans and media, who spent the next couple of weeks discussing the pros and cons of Robby's innovative dispute resolution method.

In 2005, Gordon added another asterisk to his career record book by becoming the first American to win a stage in what many consider the most grueling of motorsports, the Dakar race (formerly known as the Paris-Dakar). Robby loved the event so much that he immediately began planning to return the next year with his own team. In 2006, he took on the Dakar with his own Hummer H3 sponsored by Jim Beam and Toyo Tires. He made it through the first eight stages then had to withdraw after a large clump of grass hidden behind a huge sand dune ended his chances. He was making the treacherous Special Stage run over open desert in fading light between the oasis towns of Zouerat and Atar in Mauritania when he drove his Hummer up over a dune only to find the sandy crest breaking away underneath him. Unfortunately, instead of landing in the usual soft sand on the other side, Robby's Hummer struck a large patch of native plants, known as camel grass, encrusted with hard sand. The relatively minor impact pushed Hummer's front bumper bar right through the grill, puncturing the radiator. Robby was out of the running, but not before he'd made a substantial impact on the race.

When he's not actually at a NASCAR track, you'll find Robby anywhere there's a vehicle-friendly surface. One of the most versatile drivers in North America, on any given weekend Gordon drives in off-road competitions—he's a six-time off-road champion. And between his racing crews, his off-road store and his fabrication facility, the tireless wheelman also manages a staff of nearly 50 people and is respected as an absolute perfectionist. Yet even with all that responsibility, Robby Gordon never fails to take time for his fans and is one of the most popular drivers at the trackside meet-and-greets each race weekend.

Even at home, Gordon doesn't slow down. He thrives on his speed-driven hobbies, including boating, mountain biking and motorcycle riding, and he has recently added wakeboarding and sky skiing to his list of pastimes. His philosophy is to get the most out of life and never accept "no" for an answer. Robby is currently single, although he previously dated a former Miss Winston, Renee White. But because his personal time is so filled with his high-speed loves, there's not much time for real romance. He does, however, enjoy fine dining, especially when he's racing in Las Vegas, where Nobu, his favorite restaurant, is located. He also enjoys Mexican cuisine and is a huge country music fan. When he's not driving on racetracks, he gets around in his Corvette, Chevrolet Suburban or 1967 Cadillac Seville convertible.

In some 20 years of racing, Robby's track winnings have amounted to around $20 million, and even though a NASCAR championship still eludes him, Robby remains focused and determined that his expertise and persistence will pay off. We hope so too, because if anyone deserves the Cup crown, Robby "Flash" Gordon is first in line.

Chapter Fifteen

Kasey Kahne

DATE OF BIRTH: April 10, 1980

BIRTHPLACE: Enumclaw, Washington

RESIDES: Mooresville, North Carolina

DRIVES: No. 9 Dodge Dealers/UAW Dodge Charger
(Nextel series), No. 38 Lawry's/Great Clips
Dodge (Busch series)

In September 2005, the town of Enumclaw in Washington celebrated Kasey Kahne Day. Almost all of the town's modest population turned out as a street was named in honor of the young hometown stock car driver who has broken track records and hearts since he started driving in NASCAR's most prestigious series, the Nextel Cup, in 2004.

The modest 25-year-old driver, dressed in blue jeans with his shirt untucked, expressed his gratitude to the town that nurtured and supported him and promised to win another big race soon and make Enumclaw proud. The crowd responded with whoops and hollers, letting Kasey know they were with him for the long haul. That Monday,

Kasey Kahne stood surrounded by family, friends and fans enjoying the proclamations and dedications as Enumclaw officially celebrated its very own auto-racing hero. On presenting Kahne with a key to the city, the Mayor assured the crowd, "this is not a key to any lock," then went on to tell Kasey that it was "...the key to the hearts of the citizens of this city."

Kasey Kahne is enjoying every minute of it, too. In 2004, he won NASCAR's Rookie of the Year. Then, in May '05, after 46 races, six pole victories and six second-place finishes, he finally got his first big-time win in a Cup race in Richmond, Virginia. He has also achieved near rock-star status with legions of young female fans who follow his every move, running after him at the track the same way girls did 40 years ago for a certain group of young men with shaggy haircuts from England. Kahne was courted by television and appeared in several commercials, one of which pokes fun as his heartthrob image and appeal to the ladies. Even *People* magazine recently named him one of "America's Top 50 Bachelors."

Accolades and sighing girls aside, like most stock car racers, Kasey comes from a grassroots background. His first competitions took place on dirt tracks close to home. Kasey began his illustrious racing career in 1994 at age 14, winning four micro-midget events in his home state in a car prepared by his father, Kelly. Kasey won 11 of

14 mini-sprint events to earn the Hannigan (WA) Speedway championship as well as the Northwest Mini-Sprint Car championship in 1996. But like his driving, his progression in the sport was fast and furious.

By 1998, Kasey was running full-size sprint cars and visited Victory Lane a dozen times in his first season. He quickly came to the attention of Steve Lewis, who had previously employed Jeff Gordon and Tony Stewart in the driver's seat. Lewis offered Kahne a sprint, midget and Silver Crown contract that would run the full United States Auto Club (USAC) schedule.

In his first season, Kahne took the USAC (United States Autosound Competition) Silver Crown Rookie of the Year title as well as both the USAC Midget Series Champion and Driver of the Year honors. For the first time in his career, he was racing on both dirt and asphalt surfaces. Kahne competed in the Atlantic Series and a partial USAC schedule, racing occasionally with the World of Outlaws, Gumout Racing Series and All-Star Circuit of Champions winged sprint car associations. He triumphed at the Night Before the 500 Classic at Indianapolis Raceway Park in 2000 and 2001, becoming the first driver to post back-to-back victories in the annual event since Jeff Gordon did so in 1989 and 1990. The superstar earned two wins on the same night at the USAC midget series and sprint car series doubleheader at California's Irwindale Speedway in October 2001.

In 2002, Kahne signed with Robert Yates to run a limited NASCAR Busch Series Grand National Division schedule. His best finish was a 10th-place effort at Michigan International Speedway, but it didn't take the youngster long to prove his skills behind the wheel of a "grown-up" race car. Still, Kahne didn't get his first Busch Series win until the 2003 season finale at Homestead-Miami Speedway. Considering that he had previously experienced quick success at every other stage in his career, Kasey was surprised it took so long to get the Busch Series win. He expressed more relief than joy in an after-race press interview. "I really didn't think it would take so long. It did take a while, almost two years, but I did learn a lot in all that time and it actually felt that much better when we finally did win a race."

Kasey won the 2003 Jim Raper Memorial Dirt Cup at Skagit Speedway for the second consecutive year, becoming the first Washington native to win back-to-back titles at the Dirt Cup, which is held in Alger, Washington. Then, later in the year, Evernham Motorsports announced that Kahne would take over the No. 9 Dodge after its driver, the legendary Bill Elliott, announced his intentions to run a partial schedule. Ray Evernham became a great mentor and teacher for Kahne and the move proved fruitful for both driver and team.

Few new drivers have had an impact on the Nextel Cup Series the way Kahne did in 2004. At the start of the season, he was just another rookie looking to crack the top 20, but by the end of the season, Kasey Kahne was a household name and had sponsors, fans and media climbing all over themselves to get at him. Whether it was his hard-charging approach on the track or the year-long media frenzy that included Kahne being named one of "America's Top 50 Bachelors" by *People*, his popularity skyrocketed over 10 months in a way envied by Hollywood wannabes.

Kahne was thrilled to be Ray Evernham's choice to replace stock car legend Bill Elliott in the No. 9 Dodge Dealers/UAW Dodge. Although Kahne's credentials were impressive in the open-wheel ranks, he had limited experience with NASCAR racing. But Evernham saw the raw talent, similar to another young driver from the open-wheel ranks that he'd worked with before to win three championships and 47 races in the Nextel Series— Jeff Gordon.

In his first season with Evernham Motorsports in 2004, Kahne finished second five times, claimed the Bud Pole four times and notched up a total of 13 top-five finishes. He finished 13th in the season point standings and just missed making the inaugural Chase for the Nextel Cup field by only 28 points, but he was named the Raybestos Rookie of the Year. Kasey Kahne claimed his first

Nextel Cup Series victory in May 2005 at Richmond, with an impressive win from the pole. He qualified the No. 9 Dodge Dealers/UAW Dodge Charger in the top 10 in 15 starts, including two back-to-back poles at Darlington and Richmond. Kasey and his crew encountered many problems with the car during the 2005 season, resulting in a disappointing series of blowouts and DNFs and a 23rd-place ranking in the points standing.

Owner Ray Evernham made a major change to the structure of all his teams at by eliminating the crew chief position, traditionally one of the most important team members and the guy who calls the shots. Responsibility for the team now belongs to a leadership group made up of a team director, car director and engineer. This shift in focus and personnel is designed to nurture better collective thinking, decision making and intellectual motivation. Kahne has been teamed with Kenny Francis (team director), Mike Shiplett (car director) and Keith Rodden (engineer), and only a season or two will tell if Evernham's innovative move will have an impact on Kasey's driving style and results.

Off the track, Kasey has proven to be a real hero, too. He has set up the Kasey Kahne Foundation, recently teaming up with the CHD Awareness Quilt Project, a nonprofit organization dedicated to promoting public awareness of children born with congenital heart defects. Kasey helps the project by giving his time to personal appearances and family meet-and-greets, in addition to his financial support of the group's cause.

His own heart has also suffered some disappointments. He recently split from his girlfriend, Ashley, a Virginia Tech sophomore whom he dated for about nine months in 2005. Many speculated that Kasey would pop the question during the post-season, but the couple chose to go their separate ways around Christmas 2005. Before dating Ashley, Kasey was involved with Kristie Labonte, daughter of fellow Cup driver Terry Labonte.

Any lady wanting to catch this boy's eye needs to be able to cook a mean oven roast chicken, mashed potatoes and gravy, which is his all-time favorite meal. She would also need to share a passion for his favorite extracurricular activities, which include skiing, snowmobiling and fishing. Kasey also enjoys running as a way to relax and keep fit. He loves listening to country music, particularly George Strait, and his movie star heroes include Harrison Ford and Colin Farrell. His track heroes, though, are Jeff Gordon and Mario Andretti.

But the folks back in Enumclaw don't care too much about all this. When Kasey took the podium in September '05 during Kasey Kahne Day, he looked out across the crowd and saw a sea of people all paying homage to their hometown hero. As Enumclaw mayor John Wise dedicated "Kasey Kahne Drive" as the new name of a downtown thoroughfare, he announced to all, "There's no speedin' on that street," to gales of laughter. Kasey then presented a $1000 scholarship to a recent graduate of Enumclaw High School and answered questions people had written down. Yes, he said, being a star of NASCAR attracts the girls, but visiting children's hospitals and putting a smile on a kid's face feels so much better. Kasey proved that day what real heroes are made of.

Chapter Sixteen

Mark Martin

DATE OF BIRTH: January 9, 1959

BIRTHPLACE: Batesville, Arizona

RESIDES: Daytona Beach, Florida

DRIVES: No. 6 AAA Ford Fusion

The 2005 season was supposed to be Mark Martin's last year, along with Rusty Wallace, another legend and member of NASCAR's "old guard." But Mark decided to return in 2006 with an extension of his "Salute to You" tour and found a new sponsor in AAA for his Ford Fusion, owned by Jack Roush. Fans were overjoyed with the decision, and the beloved racer welcomes thousands of them to the meet-and-greets held each race weekend throughout the season for autographs and photos.

Martin is a true legend within stock car racing circles and has become one of the leading role models of the sport. He's spent 19 seasons in Cup racing, and his fourth-place finish in the 2005 points standings marked the third time he's had a top-four finish in the past four seasons, his 12th top-five finish in the final Cup point standings and his 15th top-10 finish in the last 17 seasons. Over the season, he earned 12 top-five and 19 top-10 finishes and took the checkered flag at Kansas and the Nextel All-Star Challenge.

Standing at only 5'6" and weighing in at just 150 pounds, Mark is still a giant in the eyes of racers and fans. He has had one of the most successful careers in racing history, and his 35 wins to date set him apart as the fourth most-winning driver among those currently active on the tracks. He is currently fourth in Nextel Cup's all-time standings, and his second-place finish at Homestead in November 2005 marked his 359th career top-10 and his 227th career top-five Cup finish. By the end of 2005, Martin had started 638 Cup races since he began his racing career on February 18, 1988.

The year was successful in many other ways for Martin, who added to his accolades in the Busch Series with victories at Fontana and Vegas and increased his series record to 47 victories. His pole at Richmond gave him 28 pole places in his career, tying for the Busch series record. In addition, Martin captured a record fifth championship in the International Race of Champions series. The veteran used his wins at Daytona and Richmond to bring his record total to 13 wins in the IROC series. Martin now has five championships in that series, including a record three straight championships from 1996 to 1998.

Whew…now let's take a break and look back to where it all started.

Mark began his stock car racing career at age 15 on the local dirt tracks around Arkansas, winning his first race after only three starts and taking the Arkansas state championship in his first year of racing in 1974. Long before he was of legal age, he had mastered tracks across the Midwest. He quickly moved up to the V-8 division in 1976 and began racing on harder surfaces later that year. Many wins followed, and by 1977, he started competing in the ASA series against drivers such as Rusty Wallace, Jim Sauter and Bobby Allison. He was crowned the ASA Rookie of the Year in 1977, and won three consecutive championships from 1978 through 1980.

Martin ran five NASCAR Cup races in 1981 using two of his own Buick Regals and entered his first full season in 1982. He had an impressive rookie year with eight top-10 finishes. But he never received the much-needed payment from his sponsor, and unable to finance the team himself, he had to auction off everything in his shop in April 1983. He ran a limited Cup schedule for various owners that year, but he returned to the ASA series for the 1984 through 1986 seasons and claimed another championship in 1986.

He took one more shot at NASCAR racing in 1987, driving a full-season Busch Grand National schedule. Mark's victory at Dover that year brought him to the attention of Jack Roush, who was preparing to begin his own Cup team for 1988. Roush chose Mark Martin to be his driver.

Since then, the Martin and Roush team has won just about everything but the Cup title. The team has consistently run at the front of the pack with one of the most successful race cars in stock car racing history—the No. 6 Ford. Despite coming up just short of a Cup championship, Mark has always said that the respect from those around him means more than any trophy ever could. He is known as "the racer's racer."

But Mark is also known as Dad to his five kids and is a doting husband to his wife, Arlene, who accompanies her husband to every race during the season. His son Matt is a budding racer and has his own webpage and growing fan base. The young driver is often seen at his dad's side on race days. When asked by reporters, Matt always cites his dad as his hero and the role model for his own future racing career. Having Mark Martin as both his idol and his father must be very cool for this teenager. What other kid's dad has his own museum, too?

In mid-April 2006, Mark opened a museum and gift shop in his hometown of Batesville, Arkansas. During the press conference leading up to the grand opening, Martin was quoted as saying,

"Growing up I couldn't wait to get out of Batesville and go out and see what I could do. I went off seeking my fame and fortune, and I was fortunate to work with a lot of great people and have a lot of success. Now it's time to bring all of that back home where it belongs to Batesville."

The state-of-the-art Mark Martin Museum features several of his cars, including the No. 6 Viagra Coca-Cola 600 win car, the 1990 Folgers Thunderbird, the No. 60 Win Dixie Busch car, Martin's 2005 IROC car that he used to win his record fifth championship and the 1989 Stroh's Thunderbird.

His family is extremely proud of Mark's accomplishments, but his own pride is tinged with some sorrow and regret. His father, Julian, was not able to share in all the celebrations as the museum was unveiled. The senior Martin died tragically in 1998 when the small plane he was flying crashed, killing him, his wife and 11-year-old daughter. Mark learned of the plane crash shortly after finishing second in a race at Watkins Glen, New York.

Never much of a public speaker, Mark has been forced to deal with the spotlight pointed straight in his face over the years of trophy presentations. He has finally come to terms with television reporters sticking microphones in his face as he pulls himself out of his race car in Victory Lane, and Martin now understands the importance of promoting his team and his sponsors, both on and off the track. He's also appeared in several TV commercials for his sponsors, heightening his profile and solidifying his presence as a Cup contender and the NASCAR poster boy for mature fans.

When men's sexual enhancement drug Viagra came on board as sponsor for the No. 6, he suffered a great deal of ribbing from his fellow drivers as well as becoming fodder for comedians and track-side reporters. But no matter what name is on the side or hood of his car, Mark Martin just aims for the checkered flag and drives!

Chapter Seventeen

Reed Sorenson

DATE OF BIRTH: February 5, 1986
BIRTHPLACE: Peachtree City, Georgia
RESIDES: Concord, North Carolina
DRIVES: No. 41 Target Dodge

The dark, handsome 20-year-old Sorenson has led a fast-paced life ever since he was old enough to steer his toy cars and trucks around his family's backyard. The son of a racer, Reed watched his dad race most weekends. He enjoyed being around the garage and pits, hearing the engines rev and feeling the rush of the speeding cars at the side of the track. So it was a natural progression for the youngster to follow in his father's footsteps.

His father started him off when Reed was only six years old in the quarter-midget division. Reed won nine Southeastern championships, culminating with the National Championship in 1997. In quarter midgets, he earned over 250 checkered flags and scored 15 different track records across the country. When he was just 10 years old, he set fastest time qualifying records at both the East and West National events.

Then it was on to the Legends series and further success. During his five full seasons of competition in Legends (the 5/8-scale fiberglass full-fendered versions of the famed NASCAR modifieds), Reed compiled one of the most impressive records in series history, including 84 wins, 152 top-five results and 166 top-10 finishes in 183 starts. He also became the only Legends racer ever to score a record $12,000 purse in consecutive Superbowl events in 1999 and 2000.

Moving up to the American Speed Association (ASA) series in 2002, Reed recorded seven top-10 places in just eight starts, and in 2003, at age 17, he became the youngest ASA Rookie of the Year, with seven top-five and 14 top-10 results in 17 starts. giving him a fourth place finish in the national standings. In addition, the Rookie of the Year honors brought a prize purse of $50,000.

Sorenson's success was so great that he caught the attention of race aficionados and industry insiders. Speed Channel TV personality Bob Dillner and Buddy Baker (one of stock car racing's greatest drivers and a well-known TV commentator) both recognized the young driver's talent. Both have stated how adaptable Sorenson was to the various track surfaces and venues and said that he had the patience of a veteran. Reed's talent was something that the Chip Ganassi Racing organization with

Felix Sabates (CGRFS) also recognized, and they quickly signed Sorenson to their driver development program late in 2003.

In 2004, the 19-year-old racer not only graduated from Woodward Academy in Atlanta, but Reed also spent the season pulling triple duty, contending for the ASA championship and competing in five NASCAR Busch Series races as well as running four ARCA events for CGRFS. He captured his first ARCA win in just his second start at Michigan in July, then placed second at Talladega and fourth at Charlotte. His Busch Series starts that season resulted in one top-five and three top-10 finishes, with his best finish, fourth place, coming in the final race of the season at Homestead-Miami Speedway.

Following his solid performance throughout the 2004 Busch Series season, Reed raced a full schedule in 2005, posting victories at Nashville, where he started from the pole, and Gateway in Madison, Illinois. In 35 races, he tallied 12 top-five and 19 top-10 results. He spent much of the season competing for the championship, eventually placing fourth, and contending for Rookie of the Year honors, but Cup Series driver Carl Edwards, who was competing full time in both series, edged him out for the title.

Sorenson also made his Nextel Cup debut in 2005 with a partial race schedule, but he crashed in the fall race at Atlanta and finished in 28th place in the season finale at Homestead. In July, Reed was told that he would be driving the No. 41 Target Dodge for Chip Ganassi in the Nextel Cup Series and would compete for Rookie of the Year honors in 2006. He also planned to run a full Busch Series schedule for the season.

Going into 2006, Team Target entered its fifth season in the Nextel Cup Series, led by crew chief Jimmy Elledge. If Reed's successes to date were any indication of what his future held, he seemed likely to reach Victory Lane behind the wheel of the red-and-white No. 41 Target Dodge.

In late 2004, Reed was introduced to college freshman Liz Brown, who soon became his girl-friend and race companion at just about every event. Mutual friend NCTS rookie Kyle Krisiloff introduced them in Charlotte, North Carolina, and they have become inseparable. Liz's first racing experience was at the 2005 Daytona Speedweek, and she enjoys learning more about the art and politics of the track every day from Reed. The pair owns a dog named Brutus, who also has become a race fan and accompanies the couple on race weekends.

Chapter Eighteen

Elliott Sadler

DATE OF BIRTH: April 30, 1975

BIRTHPLACE: Emporia, Virginia

RESIDES: Emporia, Virginia

DRIVES: No. 38 M&M/Pedigree Ford

Racing has long been a Sadler family sporting tradition. It all began nearly 45 years ago, when Bud Elliott, Herman Sadler and their brothers raced around Virginia short tracks long before Elliott William Barnes Sadler was born. Growing up in such a dedicated racing family, young Elliott accompanied his dad and uncles from track to track watching them compete in the weekly racing series. Sometimes Elliott would just watch or help out, and on other occasions, he would race his toy cars around the sandboxes, driving into imaginary Victory Lanes. So nobody was surprised when Elliott told his family that he too would enter the racing game and set into action dream of writing his name in stock car racing's history books.

There was never a doubt in young Elliott Sadler's mind that he would one day be a professional race car driver. From the age of five, he set his sights on the big Cup race series, and he has never faltered in his desire. Some 20-odd years later, Elliott won his first Cup race at Bristol Motor Speedway in just his 75th start on NASCAR's top circuit.

Like his father and uncle before him, Elliott got his early training on the short tracks in his home state of Virginia. Piloting his first go-kart at age seven, he won more than 200 races before graduating to the late-model stock car division, capturing several series championships to boot. By age 18, Sadler had joined the ranks of the weekly racing series, taking the track championship title at South Boston Speedway in 1995. His success in the series catapulted him into the NASCAR arena after he caught the attention of owner Gary Bechtel. Bechtel saw Elliott's potential and put him into his car in a full-season Busch Series in 1997.

Elliott burst onto the scene in his rookie year by capturing the pole for the season-opening event at Daytona International Speedway. It took him just 13 starts to win his first career Busch Series race at Nazareth Speedway in Pennsylvania, and he ended the year with three more poles and two victories at Myrtle Beach Speedway and Gateway International Raceway. Elliott finished in an impressive fifth-place position in the Busch Series championship standings and received the Busch Pole Award for the most poles won in a single season. In the 1998 season, he scored two more Busch Series wins—at Bristol Motor Speedway and North Carolina Speedway—ending his last season as a full-time Busch Series driver.

The 1999 season brought Elliott into the legendary Wood Brothers garage as the driver of their No. 21 car, and he was signed to his first full-time NASCAR Winston Cup Series ride. His first big win came in 2001 at the Bristol Motor Speedway, when he muscled his way to the front from 38th place on the starting grid, the deepest in the field from which a driver had ever won at the half-mile track. Even more importantly, Elliott's win took the Wood Brothers team back to Victory Lane for the first time since 1993.

After four successful and exciting seasons with the Wood Brothers, Elliott left to start driving for Robert Yates Racing (RYR). Sadler and RYR found a perfect sponsor in M&M's Chocolate Candies for the 2003 season, and he soon posted two pole positions at Darlington Raceway and Talladega Superspeedway. The team finished the season with two top-five and nine top-10 finishes, resulting in a 22nd-place finish in the point standings.

But 2004 proved to be Elliott's real breakout season. He scored points early at the season opening event by winning the outside pole for the Daytona 500. Later in the Speedweek session, he took the checkered flag to win the Gatorade Twin 125 qualifying event.

Success was sweet for the "Candyman," as Sadler was now dubbed by track mates and the media. His good fortune continued throughout the season as his team won at Texas Motor Speedway and then later in the season at California Speedway, clinching a position in the inaugural Nextel Chase for the Cup. He became one of only four drivers to stay in the top 10 in point standings for the entire season and rounded out the year with two wins, eight top-five and 14 top-10 finishes, landing a respectable ninth in the championship rankings.

The year 2005 marked the third season Sadler steered the No. 38 M&M's Ford for the RYR team, but although he scored four poles, no victories came his way. Still, Elliott was able to secure the 13th position in the Cup season points standing. Not too shabby.

Elliott's love life has not been as successful as his life on the track. In 2001, he proposed to longtime girlfriend, Lisa Tollett, whom he had met four years previously. Apparently, it was love at first sight for Elliott when he spotted the Food City 250 race queen at the Bristol Motor Speedway in 1997. Sadly, the engagement didn't last, but they still see each other regularly and have remained fast friends. The latest rumors from trackside at the start of the 2006 season indicate that Elliott has been seen squiring a pretty blonde, but the whispers aren't loud enough to reveal her identity.

His best four-legged friends are his pet Tennessee Walker hounds and his beagles, who often accompany him when he goes hunting or participates in his favorite water sports. Golf is also a favorite pastime for Elliott, and he has appeared on TV's golf network in a NASCAR drivers' challenge for charity. Although he acquitted himself well, he didn't stand a chance against race legends Rusty Wallace and Dale Jarrett, who knocked him out of the winner's circle. He also enjoys playing video games and hanging out with his friends at backyard barbecues. Elliott is a spokesman for NASCAR Speedparks, and appears in TV commercials for Ford and Coca-Cola.

Elliott makes sure he allows time in his busy schedule to support a charity close to his heart, the Autism Society of America. His efforts on behalf of autism research earned him a nomination for the 2003 USG Person of the Year Award and the honor of the 2003 Outstanding Young Virginian Award by the Virginia Jaycees. He was also named one of the *Sporting News'* Good Guys.

For all his machismo and competitiveness, Elliott Sadler is one big teddy bear of a guy, and fans can look forward to many more years of celebrating in Victory Lane with the Candyman.

Chapter Nineteen

Carl Edwards

DATE OF BIRTH: August 15, 1979

BIRTHPLACE: Columbia, Missouri

RESIDES: Mooresville, North Carolina

DRIVES: No. 99 Office Depot Ford (Nextel Series),
No. 60 AmeriQuest Ford (Busch Series)

For nearly a dozen years, Carl Edwards has been racing his way into stock car history with two NASCAR-sanctioned track championships, three Rookie of the Year honors and nearly 80 feature wins on both dirt and paved tracks. In 2004, Edwards raced the No. 99 Superchips F-150 to three wins, nine top-five and 10 top-10 results while finishing fourth in the overall Craftsman Truck Series point standings. Edwards made his Nextel Cup debut in August of that same year at Michigan International Speedway, finishing a respectable 10th. In his next 12 starts, Edwards racked up one top-five and five top-10 finishes, with his best effort in the Cup Series coming at the fall Atlanta race when he qualified fourth, finished third and led his first laps as a Nextel Cup competitor.

Racing is in Edwards' blood. His father, Carl "Mike" Edwards, raced modified stock cars and USAC midgets for four decades, accumulating over 200 wins at several Midwestern tracks. He helped Carl Jr. begin his own racing career in 1993 at the age of 13, driving four-cylinder mini-sprints.

In 1994, following his dad's winning ways, Edwards took the checkered flag at four feature races running on the tracks around Missouri and Illinois in the mini-sprint series. Throughout the 1995 and 1996 seasons, he collected 14 additional wins. In 1997, he switched to the dirt circuit to compete in the IMCA modified division. Carl quickly rose through the ranks and won Rookie of the Year honors in 1998 in the IMCA modified division at Capital Speedway in Holt Summit, Missouri.

Edwards moved into top gear in 1999 as he competed in the modified (two-barrel) division and the dirt late-model class at Capital Speedway. He took the flag 13 times in the modified division on his way to scoring the NASCAR Track Championship. His next challenge was NASCAR's Weekly Racing Series in 2000. In the pro-modified (four-barrel) division, Edwards won 13 feature races, was crowned Rookie of the Year and claimed the Capital Speedway Track Championship—13 is certainly a lucky number for Carl. With his racing appetite still not satisfied, in 2000, Carl competed in three Sportsman division races, winning all of them.

Between 2001 and 2003, he racked up an impressive list of wins and top-five and top-10 places in several different divisions and series as well as capturing the 2002 Baby Grand National Championship, all the while gaining popularity with fans across the country. His wide smile, dirty blond hair and model-like physique set female fans' hearts a-flutter, and he developed his trademark post-race winning backflip, much to the concern of race officials, who feared that an accident or misjudged jump might result in injury for the star driver.

In 2003, Edwards joined the prestigious Roush Racing family, driving the No. 99 Superchips Ford F-150 in the NASCAR Craftsman Truck Series. He had an amazing rookie season, capturing three wins, one pole, 13 top-five finishes, 15 top-10 results and the Raybestos Rookie of the Year award. He finished the season eighth in the point standings— a good showing for the 23-year-old driver.

Edwards kicked off his 2004 Craftsman Truck season by winning the first race at Daytona and then followed that with a win at Kansas in July and a win at Bristol in August. Carl was in the hunt for the 2004 truck championship, and in August, he got the nod from owner Jack Roush to move up to the Nextel Cup Series to finish the season in the No. 99 Ford Taurus, as well as racing in the remainder of the truck schedule. Edwards made his debut in the Cup car at Michigan, landing a 10th-place finish. Edwards joined Terry Labonte, Matt Kenseth, Rusty Wallace and Kyle Petty as one of only five active Nextel Cup drivers to finish inside the top 10 in their first career Cup start.

In 2005, Edwards did double duty, driving in the Cup Series in the No. 99 Roush Racing Ford and in the Busch Series with the No. 60 Charter Ford. Edwards thrilled race fans with a close third-place finish in the Nextel championship after figuring prominently in a number of edge-of-your-seat drag-race-style finishes during the final races in the Chase for the Cup.

At nearly every race of the season, Carl's mother waited for him at the finish line, always ready with a hug and kiss. His family is close, and Mom likes to make sure her boy is safe after each 400- or 500-mile trip. Edwards also finds hundreds of female fans waiting for him too, as the buff boyish hunk signs autographs and poses for pictures while being hugged and squeezed as hard as perennial TV favorite Bob Barker on *The Price is Right*.

Also frequently at Carl's side in Victory Lane is a beautiful blonde famous for her own sporting achievements. Although "officially" single, NASCAR's golden boy Carl Edwards has found himself a real gold-medal girlfriend. Olympic gold medallist swimmer Amanda Beard captured Carl's heart shortly after returning from her own victory at the Athens Olympics when they met through mutual friends at Fontana race track in California.

Carl's down-to-earth manner and lack of ego was attractive to the young athlete, especially combined with his competitiveness in his chosen sport. With all this in common, they have managed to carve out a supportive relationship that has enabled each to pursue their separate competitive directions while maintaining a closeness and empathy for each other's successes and disappointments.

Had it not been for stock cars, Carl would most likely have gone into the military. He has stated on several occasions that he wanted to be a pilot. He obviously has a thing for going fast—his top off-season pastimes include riding motorcycles and mountain bikes—and he also enjoys hiking in the great outdoors. He works out regularly and is on a strict dietary regimen that fortunately includes his favorite dish, salmon and rice. But he's not completely quiet and conservative. Carl's favorite singer is Eminem, and his favorite song is "Lose Yourself," the Oscar-winning song from the movie *8 Mile*.

As his next season gets off to an exciting start, race fans are hoping Carl doesn't lose himself but stays out front of the pack. They are, no doubt, wanting more backflips to applaud in Victory Lane.

Martin Truex Jr.

DATE OF BIRTH: June 29, 1980

BIRTHPLACE: Toms River, New Jersey

RESIDES: Mooresville, North Carolina

DRIVES: No.1 Bass Pro Shops/Tracker
Chevrolet Monte Carlo

The 2006 Cup field is inundated with great rookie talent, and Martin Truex Jr. is probably one of the hottest—in the looks department as well as his driving skills!

The not-so-tall but definitely dark and handsome driver of the No.1 Bass Pro Chevy Monte Carlo is the son of Martin Truex Sr., a former champion in the Busch North Series and a successful modified driver. Martin Jr. began racing go-karts at age 11, and by 1993, he was Junior Class champion at New Egypt Speedway. A year later, he won the New Jersey Championship Series at New Egypt.

At age 18, Truex began his modified career at Wall Stadium in 1998, and despite missing the first half of the season, he managed to finish sixth in points in the modified division. Martin won his first feature race on only his eighth try, and in 1999, he placed third in points at Wall Stadium, winning the prestigious Wall Stadium Turkey Derby, a race previously won by his father.

In 2000, Martin Jr. made the big move over to the NASCAR Busch North Series and finished 12th in point standings and second in the rookie points competition. His first Busch North win came in his eighth start, when he set a track record by leading the race from flag to flag at the New Hampshire International Speedway. In his second season, Martin placed eighth in the point standings, winning races at Thompson Speedway and Stafford Motor Speedway. In 20 events, Martin had garnered two wins, one pole, nine top-five finishes and 11 top-10 results. His tally included 14 top-10 starting spots in 20 qualifying attempts. Martin Jr. eventually won three races in three years with a family-owned team.

In 2002, Truex competed in the Busch North division and made four Busch Series starts. He earned a series-high six Bud Pole Awards in the Busch North Series while setting three track records. With six top-five and 11 top-10 finishes in 23 races, he finished 11th in the points standings.

Truex continued to race with his family-owned team in the North Series in 2003, winning two races while driving a limited schedule. He also drove a part-time Busch Series schedule that same year for Chance 2 Motorsports, the team co-owned by Dale Earnhardt Jr. and his stepmother, Teresa Earnhardt. He ran only 10 races that year, but he finished with consecutive second-place finishes at Rockingham and Homestead, delivering him his first top-five finishes in the racing series. As the 2004 season dawned, Truex was chosen to run his first full season in the Busch Series under the Chance 2 umbrella.

At Bristol Motor Speedway, he earned his first career Busch Series victory and later added three more victories over the next seven races, including Talladega Superspeedway and the final NASCAR event held at Nazareth Speedway. He took the lead in the championship after Nazareth, but lost out to Kyle Busch shortly after. But a series of top-five and top-10 finishes in the second half of the season allowed Truex to dethrone Busch and secure the Busch Series championship with a race to spare.

Truex stayed in the Busch Series and successfully defended his championship crown in 2005. He won the first NASCAR race held in Mexico, as well as defending his Busch wins at Talladega and Dover International Speedway. On June 1, 2005, he took his first win at Daytona International Speedway. While on his way to his second Busch Series championship, Truex made a couple of appearances in the Nextel Cup series as a relief driver for Dale Jr., who had suffered burns in a sports car accident. Later that year, Truex started his first career Cup race for Dale Earnhardt Inc. at Atlanta Motor Speedway. But although Truex had already started his first Daytona 500 in 2005, he intentionally preserved his Cup rookie status for 2006.

By associating himself with NASCAR's most popular driver, Dale Earnhardt Jr., Martin Truex Jr. has earned his own large fan following. When he entered the 2005 Nextel All-Star Challenge, it was the fan votes that put Truex into the field for the event.

Martin scored his first Cup top-10 finish at the 2005 Coca-Cola 600 with an impressive seventh-place finish. The 2006 season ushered in his first full-time race schedule in a Cup season, driving the No.1 Bass Pro Shop Chevrolet for Dale Earnhardt Inc.

When he's not on track, Martin enjoys putting his sponsor's products to good use. He's an avid fisherman and hunter and enjoys taking his four-wheelers out for off-road adventures. He is also a keen snowboarder. Like many of his fellow drivers, Martin is an avid computer gamer, especially for any game that involves speed and dexterity.

Martin is not yet married. However, in the early part of 2006, he was seriously dating Sherry Pollex. Towards the end of the 2005 season, she accompanied Martin to a few fan club events as well as on a trip New Jersey, where she met his family. Track rumors suggest it's true love for Truex and that he is getting ready to pop the question.

Never one able to keep a secret, Martin's team-mate Dale Earnhardt Jr. fuelled the engagement speculation when he announced his friend's intentions on a "One Night Stand with Dale Jr." webcast. Earnhardt confirmed that he and his friends had been taking bets on when Martin would get down on bended knee. Sherry is a communications manager for Miller High Life as well as working for an independent motorsports public relations firm. She's quite the athlete too, and she participated in the Charlotte Observer's 2005 10-kilometer Run for Peace along with Tammy Kahne, Kasey's mom. But until that ring is on Sherry's finger, Martin's legions of female fans still have their dreamy driver all to themselves.

Chapter Twenty-One

Matt Kenseth

DATE OF BIRTH: March 10, 1972

BIRTHPLACE: Cambridge, Wisconsin

RESIDES: Mooresville, North Carolina

DRIVES: No.17 DeWalt Power Tools Ford

Back in 1985, Cambridge, Wisconsin native Roy Kenseth cut a deal with his 13-year-old son Matt that would impact not only his own family, but also the stock car racing world and the fans who love the sport. He promised he would purchase a car, Matt would work on it and Roy would race it. And when Matt turned 16, he could put on his helmet and take over driving. So in 1988, at 16, Matt won his first feature event in only his third start—he was still a junior in high school. Over the next two seasons, Matt won 10 events at various Wisconsin tracks, and was racing late models by age 19. He raced against seasoned stock car vets such as Dick Trickle, Ted Musgrave (the 2005 Truck Champion) and Rick Bickle in the Wisconsin late-model ranks. He made ARTGO Challenge Series history by becoming the youngest winner ever, breaking the record set by a driver who would soon play a large part in his future— Mark Martin.

Like many young men his age, high school seemed to be an inconvenience for Matt, who once got caught skipping an English class. His teacher confronted Matt and asked him, "Do you think you'll be driving a race car for the rest of your life?" We all know the answer to that question!

Matt scored 46 victories running super-late models between 1993 and 1995, winning the Alan Kulwicki Memorial Race, two ARTGO events and the Wisconsin Short Track Series 200 in 1993. The 1993 season was special for a non-racing reason, too: Matt and his young wife Katie welcomed their son Ross in late May.

In 1994, Matt became the youngest driver ever to win the Miller Genuine Draft championships. Track titles at Madison International Speedway and Wisconsin International Raceway followed later that year. The next year saw Matt winning 15 of 60 events, and he was rewarded with a second consecutive Wisconsin International Raceway track title. This was also the year the rising young star made his first venture into the NASCAR arena, competing in the NASCAR All Pro Series.

Kenseth competed in the 1996 Hooters Series and celebrated a third-place ranking in the overall standings, following that in 1997 with a second place in the ASA series points. At that point,

Robbie Reiser, a fellow Wisconsin racer, suggested a move to the NASCAR Busch Grand National Series. Kenseth made his Busch Series debut on April 19, 1997, at Nashville Speedway and finished in 11th place. By the season's end, he had accumulated two top-five and seven top-10 results in only 21 starts. And in the Rookie of the Year standings, he ended up the "bridesmaid" in second place.

Matt's first full Busch Series season was 1998, and he scored three wins, 17 top-five and 23 top-10 finishes—the most top-10 results of any Busch driver that season. This time, he finished second in the overall standings. Matt got a taste of the big time in September of that year when he substituted at Dover Downs for the injured Bill Elliott, finishing sixth in his first Winston Cup start.

The 1999 season was another great year for Kenseth, who again found himself in the running for the Busch championship title, scoring four checkered flags, 14 top-five and 20 top-10 results and two poles. This time, he was third place in points, and he pulled double duty, taking on five Winston Cup starts driving for Roush Racing in the No. 17 DeWalt Tools Ford. Back at Dover Downs, he scored his best finish, ending up in fourth place.

It was Mark Martin who helped get Matt signed on to the famed Roush Racing organization. No one else had made any overtures, but Martin saw the potential and went to bat for him, securing a contract that would bring Matt into one of the most prestigious garages in stock car racing. Although Martin takes some credit for spotting the future star, he's quick to add that Matt's success comes from his skill as a driver.

Kenseth entered the Winston Cup Series full-time in 2000 and soon became the "golden boy" of the track. In only his 18th Cup start, Matt entered the history books when he became the first rookie ever to win the Coca-Cola 600. Over the rest of that 2000 season, he posted four top-five and 11 top-10 finishes and was awarded Rookie of the Year honors. He finished an impressive 14th in the overall series standings.

But the dreaded "sophomore slump" hit Kenseth in 2001. He went winless that year, logging six finishes in 32nd place or worse. But he did record four top-five and nine top-10 results and was able to finish 13th in the final standings, still not a bad result for the Winston Cup newcomer. Matt's team finished the season on a high note, earning three fourth-place finishes in the last six Cup races.

Matt's amazing pit crew fared well by winning the tough Unocal 76/Rockingham World Pit Crew Competition and beating out 24 of the best Winston Cup crews. In the process, the crew set a world record of 17.695 seconds. Next time you visit your local service station, get out your stopwatch and see how fast those guys work!

By 2002, however, Matt was back on track, recording five wins, 12 top-five and 20 top-10 results. This time, he also broke the top-10 barrier by finishing eighth in the overall standings, securing him and his team a nice payday at the end of the season. His crew, the DeWalt "Killer Bees" (the team's colors match the car's paint—yellow and black) won a second Unocal 76/Rockingham World Pit Crew Championship, breaking their own record with a 16.832-second pit stop.

If that was great, 2003's season was a corker! The Kenseth-Reiser-Roush combination was dynamite, and the No. 17 DeWalt Tools Ford team won the final Winston-era Cup championship in record-setting style. Although Matt only won a single race (Las Vegas), his consistency throughout the season kept him at the top of the championship points standings. He scored a series-best 23 top-10 finishes and 11 top-five results. Matt led the standings for a record-breaking 34-straight weeks and gave the Roush Racing organization its first-ever Cup title.

Matt and his team started the 2004 season in top form, winning two of the first three races of the season (Rockingham and Las Vegas). The No. 17 team looked good enough to repeat their previous year's championship run. But after qualifying for the final 10-race Chase for the Nextel Cup, the team fought hard just to finish out the remaining races, ending up a disappointing eighth in the championship point standings.

The 2005 race season brought about more discouraging finishes, and by mid-June, Matt found himself in unfamiliar territory at the back of the pack—in 24th position in the championship point standings. Now there were only 12 races left before the Chase for the Nextel Cup, which locked in the top-10 contenders. Despite a 320-point difference between him and the driver holding the 10th spot, Matt was determined to go down fighting.

Over the next dozen races, Matt fought his way back, scoring bonus points by leading 626 laps and notching up a win along with earning six top-five finishes and maintaining an average ninth-place finish. This was just enough for the team to again join the chosen few in the Chase for the Nextel Cup, and the team's Herculean effort to pull themselves up from the back of the pack paid off with a seventh-place finish in the championship point standings.

When Kenseth began driving on short tracks in Wisconsin, Robbie Reiser had been racing for some years, but the two did not get along. The rivalry between the two was so bitter that even their fathers got into the act, squaring off against each other at trackside. But Reiser gave Kenseth his first big career break when he offered Matt a ride in the Reiser's team car in the Busch Series in 1996. They are now inseparable as driver and crew chief and have proven to be a lethal combination on the track.

Wife Katie has supported Matt's career throughout his rise from short track to Nextel Cup, and she has helped him keep things in perspective, especially when Matt went through his career slump in 2001. Together, they share a wicked sense of humor that allows them to shrug off the occasional disappointments as well as cope with the stresses of constant travel while raising their son. She helps Matt relax by joining him on their boat during the brief periods of racing downtime and lets him spend "time with the boys" (his fellow drivers) out on the golf course. He also enjoys racing motorcycles and spending time with his son, Ross, dueling on computer games.

Matt and Katie also make time for their beloved cats, Lars and Charlotte—Lars is quite a character and is often mentioned during post-race interviews. Perhaps Lars may even get a special room at the new Matt Kenseth Fan Club Headquarters, located in Cambridge, Wisconsin, just outside of Madison. The facility features a museum and gift store loaded with Kenseth souvenirs. Admission is free, and visitors are welcome to take photos of the exhibits and Matt's cars.

Chapter Twenty-Two

Jimmie Johnson

DATE OF BIRTH: September 17, 1975
BIRTHPLACE: El Cajon, California
RESIDES: Charlotte, North Carolina
DRIVES: No. 48 Lowe's Chevrolet

Tall, dark and handsome, Jimmie Johnson is the poster boy for 21st century stock car racing. Since his 2002 rookie year, Johnson has continued to develop and grow as a driver. He has also attracted a huge following of female fans eager to stand in line at the trackside meet-and-greets every Sunday throughout the season. Although he recently married his long-time girlfriend, Chandra, those same fans still whistle, hoot and holler every time the No. 48 drives past the stands.

Johnson is very much a guy's racer, and thanks to the skill and shrewdness of crew chief Chad Knaus, Johnson and his team have pushed the envelope with regulations, testing the limits of acceptable adjustments. The team has been solid from the start. Even when Knaus was banned for four races from the track in early 2006 for allegedly using a device in the car that raised the back window three-quarters of an inch, giving Jimmie an aerodynamic advantage, temporary crew chief and Hendrick engineer Darian Grubb took over and helped Johnson take his first victory in the Daytona 500. The success was also the second consecutive Daytona race win for owner Rick Hendrick. With a little long-distance pre-race coaching from Knaus, Jimmie finished second in his next race at California Speedway and then beat out Matt Kenseth by a mere half-car length to win the third race of the season in Las Vegas.

Johnson had carved out a fast career track, and at the start of 2006, he appeared destined to figure prominently in future Cup championships. At the end of 2005, for the fourth consecutive year, Jimmie finished in the top five in the Chase for the Cup. The finish also marked the second time in as many years that Johnson and his Lowe's team were in contention to win the championship going into the final race of the season.

While Jimmie and his team have made it look easy, it took a lot of hard work and dedication to bring him into the elite circle of Nextel Cup superstars. Like most of his peers, Jimmie began racing at about the same time he started school. With his family's support, he rode his first 50cc motorcycles at age five. With younger brothers Jarit and Jessie tagging along and his father, Gary, and mother,

Cathy, cheering his every move, Jimmie spent most weekends camping and racing.

His early days on a motorcycle brought Jimmie his first championship. He won the 60cc class championship at age eight despite blowing out his knee with several races still remaining in the season. He soon graduated from motorcycles to the Mickey Thompson Entertainment Group (MTEG) Stadium Racing Series, winning more awards and gaining attention from fans and the media.

In 1993, Jimmie's racing mentor, supercross champion Rick Johnson (no relation), arranged a meeting that would prove fortuitous for the eager youngster. While Jimmie was racing at the Los Angeles Coliseum, Rick introduced him to the Executive Director of GM Racing, Herb Fishel, who saw first-hand Jimmie's racing potential. Fishel monitored Johnson's progress throughout the year and eventually persuaded GM's off-road racing team Johnson was the fellow they needed to drive their car.

Johnson jumped at the opportunity and spent the next few years driving everything he could lay his hands on in off-road stadium and desert races. He also proved to be a savvy businessman and self-promoter, always learning and improving his ability to connect with fans and potential sponsors by taking on color commentary duties for ESPN in the Short Course Off-Road Drivers Association (SODA) series.

All the hard work and long hours on and off the track paid off when Johnson met his future car owners, Stan and Randy Herzog. Jimmie created his own proposal and took it to his friend, Fishel, who gave the owners and their new, ambitious driver a chance at the brass ring. Johnson climbed into an American Speed Association car in 1997 and got his first taste of pavement racing. In 1998, he started three Busch Series races—Indianapolis Raceway Park, Gateway International Raceway and Homestead Miami Speedway—and finished fourth in the ASA national championship points race during his first full season, earning him ASA's Pat Schauer Memorial Rookie of the Year. Jimmie's string of victories in the ASA Series accelerated his move up to NASCAR in what has quickly become one of the most exciting new careers in Busch and Nextel Cup racing.

Jimmie entered the Busch Series in 1999 with a personal-best finish of seventh place in his first start at the Milwaukee Mile. In 2000, he finished 10th in the Busch Series and had three sixth-place finishes. Finally, in 2001, Jimmie took his first trip to Victory Lane, winning at the Chicagoland Speedway and finishing out the year with four top-five and eight top-10 finishes. He made three Winston Cup Series starts in 2001 for car owners Jeff Gordon and Hendrick Motorsports. But in his first Winston start, he qualified 15th and finished a humbling 39th.

Jimmie took the step to Cup racing in 2002, an amazing rookie year. He visited Victory Lane three times and notched up 21 top-10 results, finishing fifth in the overall series. He also scored four Bud Poles (Daytona, Talladega, Lowe's Motorspeedway and Richmond International) and was the first rookie in history to win both season races at Dover and the lead in the points standings. But even with such an astounding debut, Jimmie ended up losing Rookie of the Year to Ryan Newman.

The No. 48 Lowe's team enjoyed even more success in 2003 with Jimmie winning two Bud Pole Awards at Pocono and Kansas, making three more trips to Victory Lane and earning 14 top-five and 20 top-10 finishes. He nailed the all-star race at Lowe's Motorspeedway, winning the huge purse of $1 million, and finished second in the season's points standings.

The 2004 season was another great year to remember with one Bud Pole at the Coca-Cola 600 on May 30, 2004, and two other poles received because of rained-out conditions that meant owner points determined the races when Jimmie was leading the standings. He won an amazing eight events, four of which came during the Chase for the Cup, and took 13 top-five and 10 top-10 finishes. Jimmie swept Darlington, Pocono Raceway and Lowe's Motorspeedway, winning both races held at each track for the season. He also led the championship points starting at race 15 of the season on June 20 for eight consecutive weeks, and then led the points for one more week for the last time after race 25. But he was the "bridesmaid" again, finishing the year as number two in points just a mere eight points behind leader Kurt Busch. The newly introduced Chase for the Cup format worked out well for the Lowe's team, and the championship was the closest it had been in years, coming down to the last race at Miami-Homestead to determine the series winner.

Although he didn't take home the Cup, Jimmie did win a big prize—he married his girlfriend of two years, Chandra Janway, on December 11, 2004. Chandra had been a constant presence during race season, sharing Jimmie's victories and helping him settle into a focused racing rhythm. She was always there cheering him on and has proven to be a wonderful partner with his various charitable endeavors.

Early in 2006, Jimmie and Chandra announced the creation of the Jimmie Johnson Foundation to aid charities working with children and families. During the press conference, Jimmie said, "This is the culmination of a lot of hard work and thought by a lot of people. [Chandra and I] get to do what we enjoy doing in life. Not everyone is as fortunate. So we wanted to give something back. [We] decided we wanted to help families, particularly children." The foundation's mission is to initially fund five charities: the American Red Cross, the Victory Junction Gang, the Randy Dorton Memorial Fund, the Make-A-Wish Foundation and the Hendrick Marrow program. The foundation's first fundraising activity was an online charity auction that featured racing and sports memorabilia, including much of Jimmie's autographed racing gear.

Jimmie and Chandra share their Charlotte, North Carolina home with their dogs, Roxanne (Shih Tzu) and Maya (Havenese). Both dogs are featured in the Greg Biffle Foundation's 2006 calendar of NASCAR drivers and their pets.

Chapter Twenty-Three

Dale Jarrett

DATE OF BIRTH: November 26, 1956

BIRTHPLACE: Newton, North Carolina

RESIDES: Hickory, North Carolina

DRIVES: No 88 UPS Ford

D ale Jarrett was born to race, although that was a fact he discovered late. His father Ned was a two-time NASCAR championship winner who retired in 1965, when Dale was still a child. Dale grew up playing alongside Richard Petty's son Kyle at the tracks each week, but to him, the race-track was just where dad worked and where he got to play. Racing was not his future, at least in his young eyes.

Dale, or "D.J.," was quite the young jock in high school, lettering in football, basketball, baseball and golf, a pastime that has since become his off-track passion. But for all his competitiveness, he still lacked focus. Jarrett turned down a golf scholar-ship at the University of South Carolina, but he still didn't see racing anywhere in his future, nor did he see settling down to a regular nine-to-five existence. Dale had tried domesticity, but soon after his son Jason was born in 1975, he and the baby's mother divorced.

He shuffled between jobs, sometimes working for the family lumber business, then as a car salesman, and he even tried his hand as a printing press operator. Fortunately, though, his father was the track promoter at Hickory Motor Speedway. Dale took on a variety of jobs there, including taking tickets, working concession stands, driving the pace car and even mowing the infield and apron grass in order to make child support payments and build a nest egg for whatever career endeavors were next on the list.

Then, one night in 1977, Dale had an epiphany while working at Hickory—he would be a stock car driver, and he was determined to be one of the best. From that night onwards, he practiced, he raced and he practiced some more. Jarrett spent many years as a journeyman driver, accepting rides from whoever would offer, and racing in the Limited Sportsman Division at his hometown track, Hickory Motor Speedway. Just as he had in other sports, Dale displayed a determination that would carry him through the lean times—and there were many. He finally made his full-time Busch Grand National debut in 1982, followed by his Winston Cup debut in 1984 at Martinsville, but it wasn't until 1987 that he drove more than a few races in a season.

In 1988, he was hired to share driving duties with Cale Yarborough, who was driving a limited schedule on his way to retirement, but Dale lost his ride at the end of the next year. Throughout the '80s, Dale continued to compete in the NASCAR Busch Series, which ran at various tracks, located primarily in the Southeast, as a companion series to the Winston Cup Series at several venues. While Dale yearned to compete in "the big race" on Sundays, he understood the value in spending time behind the Busch Series wheel. His time in the lower ranks would give him entry into the Winston Cup, and it would help develop the skills and race strategies he needed to succeed at the top level.

His big break came early in 1990, when he received a call from the legendary Wood Brothers, NASCAR's oldest and most respected team. Jarrett was asked to take over the wheel of the No. 21 Ford about five races into the 1990 season for Neil Bonnett, who was injured in a crash at Daytona. Dale showed signs of brilliance throughout the year and secured the ride full time for the 1991 season. Jarrett scored the first win of his NASCAR Winston Cup career in the 1991 fall event at Michigan International Speedway. But that same weekend, Dale announced that he would be driving the following year for a start-up team headed by Joe Gibbs, who was leaving the NFL to start up a new NASCAR team. Dale and his new his wife Kelley thought long and hard over the decision to leave the Wood Brothers to join a new and untried operation, but Gibbs exuded charisma and a spiritual strength that convinced the Jarretts to make the move. The switch also allowed Dale the opportunity to work with his brother-in-law, Jimmy Makar, who was a much-respected chassis man.

By the time he left Wood Brothers Racing at the end of 1991, DJ had earned 15 top-10 places for the team. After joining the Gibbs organization, he scored another eight top-10 results in the first year with his new team, and he started 1993 off with a bang by winning the Daytona 500, out-driving stars such as Dale Earnhardt and Jeff Gordon. He went on to accumulate 13 top-five and 18 top-10 finishes that year, securing a fourth-place finish in the points standings by season's end. Unfortunately, DJ dropped to back into 16th in the 1994 standings, prompting his decision to leave Gibbs and form his own team.

Several other drivers have taken on owner-driver responsibilities and experienced success, although the costs involved are exorbitant. While Dale was pondering the business move, Robert Yates, the renowned engine builder and car owner, was experiencing a successful run with driver Ernie Irvan. But an ill-fated accident at Michigan threatened to end Irvan's career, sidelining him for the remainder of 1994 and through most of the 1995 season. The crash left Yates looking for a driver for his No. 28 Ford for the 1995 season.

Although the No. 28 driver's seat contract was only a one-year deal, Dale saw endless opportunities in driving for Robert Yates Racing. He could learn from Yates and build on that knowledge when he formed his own Cup team beginning in 1996. But as the season progressed, both Jarrett and Yates realized that they might want to extend their relationship past the contract deadline and into 1996. Jarrett made a great first impression on RYR when he won the pole for the Daytona 500, and later that summer, he had just enough fuel to cross the finish line at Pocono in July to give him his first win for Yates. He also scored nine top-five and 14 top-10 finishes by season's end. Rather than lose Jarrett's burgeoning talent, Yates decided to expand to a two-car operation, adding the No. 88 Ford with Jarrett as the driver.

The start of the1996 season brought Jarrett and RYR unimaginable success for a first-year team. With guidance from crew chief Todd Parrott, Jarrett won the 1996 Bud Shootout at Daytona. A week later, Jarrett almost repeated his 1993 win exactly in the Daytona 500 by beating Earnhardt again to the checkered flag for his second victory in the season-opening event. Jarrett finished out 1996 with three more wins, including the prestigious Brickyard 400 at Indianapolis Motor Speedway. He racked up a final tally of 17 top-five and 21 top-10 finishes, securing a career-best third in the point standings and establishing the No. 88 team as a future championship contender.

The following year, he finished a mere 14 points behind the winner of the Cup, Jeff Gordon. In 1999, all his hard work and determination paid off with the Winston Cup championship, making Dale and Ned Jarrett the first father-son combination to win titles since Lee and Richard Petty. That year also brought him his highest payday to date, with over $6.6 million in winnings for the season.

In 2000, the Daytona 500 trophy was Dale's for the third time when he won from the pole and collected a paycheck of more than $2 million. He scored another win that season in addition to 15 top-five and 24 top-10 results before finishing the year fourth in the final point standings, earning just under the $6 million mark.

UPS took over primary sponsorship of Jarrett's No. 88 team at the start of the 2001 season and created a fun promotion for the fans called "Race the Truck." Dale's popularity soared at the tracks with fans of all ages asking him when he will race the big, brown UPS courier truck. With a fifth-place finish in Cup standings, perhaps he wished that he had raced that truck instead of the No. 88.

The 2002 season saw a further slip in the points standings with a ninth-place finish and a drop in earnings to around the $4 million mark. But it was the 2003 season that nearly broke the team. After winning at Rockingham early in the year, Jarrett managed only five more top-10 finishes that year, and to add insult to injury, he finished outside the top 20 some 21 times, including nine races when he failed to even finish. The final standings showed him in 26th position, but thanks to inflation and increased sponsorships, his earnings were higher the previous year's mark, and he ended up taking home just over $4 million.

DJ returned in 2004 determined to prove the previous year was an aberration and started off by taking the top honors for the third time at the Budweiser Shootout. He beat out two of the young guns, Kevin Harvick and Dale Earnhardt Jr., fighting them for position over the last seven laps of the race after a late-race restart. Jarrett finally pulled ahead to lead the last lap of the invitation-only event and crossed the finish line about two car lengths ahead of Earnhardt. The rest of the season, however, was a complete bust, with DJ failing to win a race for the first time since 1992. He scored six top-five and 14 top-10 results, finishing 15th in the 2005 points standings.

Jarrett's 2005 season was another stinker with his second consecutive 15th place finish in the Cup standings, leaving the entire RYR organization disappointed and in need of a real shake-up. Dale's team went through two crew chief changes during the season, finally bringing in "Slugger" Labbe (who has played an important part in previous championship-winning teams) to work with DJ going into the 2006 season. There were a few bright spots in the dismal '05 calendar, most notably a victory at Talladega late in the season that snapped DJ's 98-race winless streak. Apart from the win, the team scored one pole, four top-five and seven top-10 finishes plus two DNFs. But the Talladega win was without a doubt the high-light of Jarrett's season: it was the 32nd victory of his career and his 30th behind the wheel of a Ford.

The 2006 NASCAR season marked Jarrett's 20th year of racing, his 12th with Robert Yates Racing and the sixth with UPS on board as primary spon-sor. And with Slugger helming the team from the pit box, Dale is looking forward to getting back into the Chase for the Cup.

He no longer considers the possibility of own-ing his own team, though, especially at racing's highest level. In recent years, he has found that he'd rather devote his time and energy to his family and his home back in Hickory, where he was raised. Jarrett and his wife Kelley are active philanthropists, supporting several charitable organizations. Their children, Jason, Natalee, Karsyn and Zachary, are all active in sports them-selves, and DJ is proving a proud and supportive father, like his dad was for him.

Dale and Kelly are starting to enjoy more time together off the track, playing golf and watching TV, especially reruns of *Home Improvement* (DJ's favorite show) and lots of pro football. He's happy to give Kelly the remote so she can plug in and watch their favorite movie, *Titanic*. The Jarrett family has two beloved pets, a Siamese cat named Samantha and a Labrador retriever named Zoe.

Dale is planning on making a lot more time for his family in the next few years. At the spring '06 Bristol race, he announced that he would retire after the 2008 Nextel Cup season. Stock car racing's loss will probably be golf's gain, as Dale has already been seen sizing up some new clubs.

Chapter Twenty-Four

The Crazy Canucks

Money makes the world go around...and it also makes the cars go around the track. In Canada, unfortunately, that seems to be the biggest obstacle stock car racers encounter. Sponsors seem to have their own restrictor plates placed firmly on their checkbooks, and many brilliant young drivers are going unnoticed because of a lack of funding for their rides.

The average cost to run a car for a full season of 11 races (excluding road races) in the CASCAR (Canadian Association for Stock Car Racing) Super Series is approximately $250,000, or $150,000 for the Ontario-only six-race schedule—chump change by NASCAR standards. But for some reason, advertisers and agencies haven't discovered the value of having their logos plastered across the movable billboards that repeatedly flash in front of thousands of consumers' eyes for up to three hours at each event—let alone the exposure on haulers, track billboards, merchandise and PA announcements.

Granted, Canada is a huge country with isolated fan clusters across the various provinces and a racing season dictated by a sometimes-unforgiving northern climate. But hockey is not the only sport in the Canadian vocabulary, and hopefully, with the increased media presence and high profile of NASCAR, those living north of the 49th parallel will get behind Canadian drivers and track promoters and give some teeth to CASCAR.

Michael Gold

One of the hottest young Canadian drivers racing the circuit is 23-year-old Michael Gold, who races the No. 97 Gold Racing Dodge and the No. 39 Dodge Charger for Whitlock Motorsports. Currently based in Sault Ste. Marie, Ontario, Michael is a second-generation driver (dad Allan Gold runs the family racing business, Gold Racing, out of London, Ontario) and is currently studying for his automotive engineering degree. Michael spent many childhood hours helping his father work on cars, learning the business from the inside out.

After taking time away from the track to establish his racing business, Gold Sr. returned to active racing halfway through the 1998 season. By 1999, young Michael caught the bug, trying out a factory-stock 1978 Monte Carlo. Michael raced a season and a half in the factory-stock division at Laird International Speedway, but he still spent lots of time in the garage working on the family's race cars. When he'd done all the work on his own car, he'd then work on his father's super-late model.

Towards the end of Michael's second season, his dad bought a new super-late model, giving Michael the opportunity to race in that division and compete against his old man. At 18 years old, he was performing well. In his second race in a super-late model, he and his father competed in a 50-lap feature at Kinross International Speedway. Michael qualified fourth, just a few hundredths of a second faster than his father's time. Gold Sr. was taken out early in a racing incident, but Michael kept his head and ended up with an impressive second-place finish, starting his super-late model career with one heck of a big bang.

Seeing the potential his enthusiastic son possessed, Allan Gold stepped down as driver to take on the role of crew chief for Michael. The Golds capped the 2002 season by taking the championship and Rookie of the Year honors.

In order for Michael to gain experience and seat time, the Golds went to Onaway Speedway in Michigan. With only one session of hot laps, Michael clocked the fastest qualifying time and a third-place finish in the feature at his first appearance on the track.

But lack of funding let the air out of the Gold racing tires—figuratively speaking—and they were only able to raise enough money to race half the

2003 season back at Laird International Speedway. Still, Michael was frequently the fastest qualifier, setting and then resetting track records in the qualifying races.

In 2004, the father-son combination worked magic on the track, and Michael captured the championship at Laird International Speedway, winning 20 races with a record of eight feature wins. Throughout the year, he was still a student in Windsor, Ontario (across the river from Detroit, Motor City, USA), and his championship point lead was so large that he didn't even have to leave school to run the last race of the season.

Throughout his 2003 and 2004 record-breaking seasons, Michael came to the attention of Canadian auto-racing media. Thanks to his good looks, clean racing and calm demeanor both on- and off-track, he was dubbed "The Tall Cool One" and "Golden Boy" by the press. He was also well respected by his fellow racers and was rewarded with the Most Sportsmanlike Driver honors at Laird in 2003.

Michael could be considered Canada's answer to Carl Edwards, but sadly, it's simply the lack of funding that prevents him and his fellow racers from finding the promotional opportunities and exposure to propel them into the same arena of stardom as Edwards and the young superstars of NASCAR.

"I think it is great how NASCAR has expanded over the last few years," Michael commented recently, "and I believe that CASCAR can create that same hype and interest in the Canadian fans. But it's in major need of more big companies stepping up and sponsoring race cars. I believe that these companies may be hesitant due to the minimal exposure we have on TV."

He went on to comment on the behind-the-scenes shows for the Nextel and Busch Series that the U.S. networks produce in support of the sport: "I really enjoy all the new shows they have profiling teams in the Busch and Nextel Cup series. I believe shows like this would be equally as successful for the Canadian drivers and help create more CASCAR fans who enjoy watching races when they know the personalities of the drivers. The PowerWater series should get more exposure as well. We had so many exciting and entertaining races, but since we weren't broadcast anywhere on Canadian television, nobody saw the amazing driving, the thrills and excitement we all experienced."

Now, with his new 20-year-old crew chief, Jacob Porco, Michael's team in the pits works incredibly hard for the race team. Gold Racing is working on a deal to run the full 2006 and 2007 seasons in the late model division at Michael's hometrack in Sault Ste. Marie. Although the team's hopes were high for running the full 2006 CASCAR Super Series, no sponsorship deals came through. For the young racer, it was extremely disappointing—he knows he can race up front—but now it seems like his career is on hold for a little while longer.

One of Michael's peers, though, was able to escape the sponsorship shackles and has been enjoying a ride on the fast track.

Pete Shepherd

Pete Shepherd, another Ontario native (from the city of Brampton, just outside of Toronto), was driving the Canadian race circuit in the No. 50 Dodge Charger for the ATTO race team when he was selected out of nearly 1700 applicants to participate in the Jack Roush "Gong Show," a selection process Roush hosts and funds that awards the winning candidate a sponsored ride in the Craftsman Truck series. Pete was selected as one of the top-25 drivers to compete in the three-week contest held at the Martinsville and Darlington tracks.

Not only did the 19-year-old impress Jack Roush, the "Cat in the Hat," but Shepherd also caught the eye of NASCAR's own Golden Boy, Carl Edwards, who in early 2006 was close to signing Shepherd as his driver in the Edward's USAC Silver Crown Series sprint car. Roush quickly signed Pete to a development deal, and the young Canadian should be driving a number of the ARCA races throughout the 2006 season. Way to go, Petey!

Hopefully, Shepherd's future successes will shine a light on the talent driving CASCAR circuits across Canada. We may soon get to see a red-and-white checkered flag wave proudly from our TV screens!

Notes On Sources

Athlon Sports Racing Magazine. Official website.
www.athlonsports.com

AutoRacing1.com. www.autoracing1.com.

CASCAR Racing. Official CASCAR website.
www.cascar.com.

CNN Sports. www.sportsillustrated.cnn.com.

Cup Scene Daily News. www.cupscene.com.

ESPN. www.espn.go.com/auto/nascar/.

Fox Sports. www.foxsports.com.

Gold Racing. Official website. www.goldracing.com

Gordon, Jeff and Eubanks, Steve. *Jeff Gordon: Racing Back to
the Front – My Memoir*. New York: Atria, 2003.

Hendrick Motorsports. Official Website. www.hendrickmo-
torsports.com.

Inside Track Magazine. Official website www.insidetrack-
news.com

Miller, Timothy & Milton, Steve. *NASCAR Now*. Richmond
Hill, ON: Firefly Books, 2004.

Motorsport.com. www.motorsport.com.

NASCAR.com. Official NASCAR website. www.nascar.com.

Racing Milestones News. www.racingmilestones.com.

Penske Racing. Official website. www.penskeracing.com.

Roush Racing. Official website. www.roushracing.com.

SpeedTV. www.speedtv.com.

Sports Illustrated. www.si.com.

White, Ben and Kinrade, Nigel. *NASCAR Racers: Today's Top
Drivers*. St. Paul, MN: Crestline, 2004.